TROPICAL SON

Essays on the Nature of Florida

JONATHAN HARRINGTON

NEWTECH PUBLICATIONS

METRO™ MAGAZINE

Published by NewTech Publications
1330 Palmetto Avenue
Winter Park, Florida 32789

CONTENTS

ACKNOWLEDGMENTS

*H*istorical and biological data in this book were gleaned from a variety of sources. For much of the material concerning the flora and fauna of Florida, I consulted the interpretive markers throughout the state and national park system, especially for data on the Florida black bear, and the manatee, as well as information on the settlement of the Blue Spring area. For material about Canaveral National Seashore, ranger Elizabeth Dupree and the *Official Map and Guide* were helpful. For information on Bok Tower Gardens I referred to the *Visitor Map & Guide* and *Bok Tower Gardens* (produced by John W. Caldwell and published by the American Foundation, Inc.). For material concerning the process of wine-making, the slide presentation, handouts, and pamphlets from Lakeridge Winery in Clermont were helpful. Ralph Costa, Mitch Cohen, and Jim Thorsen provided valuable information on the red-cockaded woodpecker.

I have also quoted briefly from Marjorie Kinnan Rawling's *Cross Creek* (Charles Scribner's Sons), R.J. Longstreet's *Birds in Florida* (Trend House), *Insight Guide of Florida* (Prentice Hall), *Atlas of Florida* edited by Edward A. Fernald (Florida State University Foundation, Inc.), *Florida Archaeology* by Jerald T. Milanich and Charles H. Fairbanks (Academic Press), *Letter at the End of Winter* by Don Stap (University of Central Florida Press), *A Parrot Without a Name* by Don Stap (Alfred A. Knopf), and *The Last Lords of Palenque: The Lacandon Mayas of the Mexican Rain Forest* by Victor

Perera and Robert D. Bruce (Little, Brown).

Many people have helped and advised me along the way as I poked around the Central Florida outdoors over the last couple years. I want to thank Bill Marino, who was my editor at *METRO* Magazine for two years. I also wish to thank *METRO* vice president of sales and marketing Michael J. Buchowski, marketing director Louise Kennedy, Editorial Director Carole Engle-Avriett, staffers Carol Barfield, Ellen Ronshagen, Theresa Swanson, Kathleen Todd, and Marita Young (who typed portions of the manuscript), and of course, Marc H. Young, the publisher of *METRO*, where all but three of these essays originally appeared. Special thanks to Fred Abel, who wore many hats on this project: editor, designer, creative director, and friend.

Mike Murphy of the *Orlando Sentinel* published "Summer of the Moon Launch" and "Native's Euphoria" in a slightly different form. "A Distant November" appeared in the *Florida Catholic*. Thanks to Gwen Thomas, formerly of *Pencil Press Quarterly*, for introducing me to the folks at *METRO*. I would also like to thank Erwin Cohen for his advice and counsel, as well as the many readers of *METRO* who have written to me.

Thanks to Jim Curtis for the back-cover photo, Rhetta Patten for the cover art, and Charles Ronshagen for the map. My colleagues Russ Kessler and Richard Adicks at the University of Central Florida read some of these pieces and made suggestions for changes, for which I am grateful. Other suggestions were made by Anne Lawrence, Omar S. Castañeda, and Stephen Becker. However, I am solely responsible for any errors or inaccuracies that occur in the book.

Thanks and appreciation to my family for its love and support, and to the memory of my parents. Finally, I dedicate this book to the little bird who flew into my life—and with her singing continues to inspire me—my wife, Wren.

INTRODUCTION

Nearly forty million tourists come to Florida each year, but few pause to see my part of the state as they roar through on the Sunshine State Parkway or Interstate 75, enroute to the glittering coasts or to the various attractions for packaged holidays. Newcomers to the state, as well as some not-so-newcomers, rarely realize that beyond the glittering facade that they see as Florida, there is another Florida of small towns, coastal villages, farms, ranches, rivers, springs, caves, deserted beaches, and hidden coves. Sadly, it is a Florida that is rapidly disappearing.

I am a rare bird since I am among the twenty-two percent of Florida's citizens considered "natives" by birth. My accent is unmistakably Southern; I was twenty-one when I first saw snow, and I have lived much of my life in rural Florida, within an hour's drive of both the Gulf and Atlantic coasts.

During my brief sojourn in the North, I told people about my Florida, but because so few people had seen or heard of the places I described, I think they doubted their existence. Little wonder, then, that I too began to believe that the home I remembered was just a dream, inspired by my own romantic notions of an earthy, subtropical backwater.

The Florida where I was born and raised lies in the
center of the sprawling, pan-flat peninsula. Get off the
major highways and out of the cities, and you will see
vestiges of my Florida: orange groves, their blossoms
deliciously fragrant in spring; green pastures studded
with cabbage palms; and crystalline lakes bordered by
subtropical growth.

Drive an hour and a half north of Orlando, and you
are in the Ocala National Forest, the only subtropical
forest in the United States. Southwest of Orlando are the
vast, low wetlands of the Green Swamp, a wilderness of
dense, humid forests. When I was a teenager, a "wild
man" was found in the Green Swamp who lived on
armadillos. All this, mind you, in the shadow of Cape
Kennedy, where the first men were sent to the moon in
1969.

No other state has so carefully constructed an image
of itself to project to the rest of the nation than Florida.
Perhaps no place contradicts that image of a sunny
paradise more dramatically than my Florida. In a state
that boasts of being the fastest growing in the nation, it
is as though some parts of Florida are just awakening
from a long primordial sleep. Vestiges of the Old South
are still present in many parts of rural Florida. But
Florida is different from the South.

What makes it different? First, there is the climate.
Until the disastrous freezes of 1983, 1985, and 1989,
Central Florida dominated the world of citrus produc-
tion because of its subtropical weather. Summers are
long and often hot, although they are tempered by breezes
from both the Gulf of Mexico and the Atlantic Ocean.
Parts of Central Florida are situated on the Ridge—a
strip of land that "soars" to over 300 feet above sea level.
In a state of low relief such as Florida, the Ridge seems
in parts like our own version of the Andes.

Combined with warm weather and high rainfall (ironically, the Sunshine State is the second most rained upon

state in the nation), the Ridge presents the ideal conditions for growing oranges, grapefruit, tangerines, and other tropical fruits. As a result, it contained until recently the densest concentration of citrus trees in the world.

The people are different here, too. Again, the environment engenders this difference. Florida is a region of water. So the native is often a fisher. He likes freshwater bass and catfish, rolled in cornmeal and fried in oil, with hushpuppies and yellow grits. If offered fresh shrimp, blue crab, oysters, and other fare from the nearby coasts, he accepts them with delight.

Fruits and vegetables are also plentiful and fresh, year-round. The outdoor produce stand, sometimes consisting of no more than the back of a pickup truck and a hand-lettered sign advertising watermelons, cucumbers, tomatoes, mangoes, papayas, oranges, avocadoes, grapefruit, and a variety of other locally grown products, is an institution found on almost every back road. Not to mention the ubiquitous "hot-boiled peanuts."

But change is coming quickly, even to the remote areas of Florida. I find, in my own hometown, an influx of newcomers. When I ask if they have been here long, some reply, "Yes, I've been here seven months."

There are places in Florida that are among the most beautiful on this earth. Many of these places are in danger of being spoiled, and I tell you about them with the 'fear that your knowing of their existence might actually lead to their demise. You may say that you would never move into a swamp. Yet many of Florida's cities were built directly on drained swamps in the days before developers were aware of the importance of wetlands.

I am not opposed to controlled, sensible growth. Anyone who has ever dreamed of living in a tropical paradise would find my part of Florida an acceptable compromise. But we must always keep in mind the sad irony of development—the more people who come to get away from it all, the more likely that the place they have come to will become like the place they have fled. I hope that if you will learn to recognize the unique and fragile beauty of a swamp, if you will learn to see a tract of wiry scrub as a rich habitat for unusual and endangered plants and animal species, if you will look into the eyes of an alligator and see, not a horrible, dangerous monster, but a precious link to our prehistoric past, you will learn to enjoy Florida and become as protective of her as I am.

So follow me in this book on a journey into the heart of the real Florida, where nature offers attractions more magical than any human could ever devise. Hike with me into the subtropical forests, dive into clear springs, stroll along deserted beaches, and canoe Florida's wild rivers. I hope that someday, when you love her subtropical shores as dearly as I, you will come to think of her as "our Florida."

WEKIWA
TRAIL

*T*here seems to be an uneasy alliance in Florida between "natives" and "newcomers." The natives sport "native" license plates and recall the way things used to be. The "newcomers" are quick to invoke the phrase, "but back up North...." Extremists on both sides seem certain that they have nothing to learn from each other. I disagree.

If I told you that three miles from State Road 436 (that epitome of commercialism) there is a pristine, subtropical wilderness teeming with whitetail deer, wood storks, black bear, raccoons, the endangered gopher tortoise and cotton mouse, herons, egrets, pileated woodpeckers, barred owls, and crystalline springs, you might not believe me. What if I told you that you can easily enter this wilderness area, leave the jammed traffic of 436, experience a beautiful state recreation area, and by hiking anywhere along a thirteen-mile trail, leave the 20th century behind?

You can have this glimpse of natural Florida without leaving metropolitan Orlando by visiting the 6,400-acre Wekiwa Springs State Park. This park illustrates the inherent contradiction of Florida. That is, a rapidly developing state in which four-fifths of the population live in urban areas, yet a state with a uniquely beautiful and fragile natural environment. Ancient stands of cypress trees and untouched swamps may lie within a stone's throw of a major shopping mall. The point is to be able to recognize these undeveloped areas as rich habitats for plant and animal life, not merely empty land to be exploited.

One spring I took a hike with a friend of mine from England on the Wekiwa Springs State Park Hiking Trail. This is part of an extensive system of trails, developed by the Florida Trail Association, that winds through some of the most unspoiled parts of the state. I wanted to show her part of my Florida.

We started hiking in the crisp mid-morning from a point near the spring. "Wekiwa" is from the Creek Indian word meaning "spring of water." Wekiwa Springs is formed by water surging up from underground limestone caverns. This spring is the source of the Wekiwa River, which joins Rock Springs Run on its journey to the St. Johns River, fifteen miles to the northeast. The river can be explored by canoes that are rented at the state park for a reasonable fee. By canoe, one can observe alligators, raccoons, otters, and a host of wading birds, as the river winds through lush subtropical wilderness.

We stepped onto the wooden bridge that arches over Wekiwa Spring and entered a wilderness which, in many respects, is unchanged from the time Ponce de Leon first set foot on the Florida peninsula in 1513.

Near the spring the trail was damp and spongy. Sabel palms towered over us, and the dense vegetation of laurel oaks, water oaks, sweetbay, and other hardwoods created a damp, shady area. These shady areas within the forest are known as hammocks, areas of deep humus-rich soil that are slightly higher than the surrounding forest and are characterized by stands of hardwoods. Our word "hammock" (unlike the thing you sleep in)

comes from the Seminole Indian word for "shady place."
Here, a small, circular nature trail takes you through
the hammock. The Hammock Trail has even been modi-
fied to accommodate blind persons. Its interpretive
markers explaining the flora and fauna also appear in
Braille. This reminded us that we should rely on all of
our senses when exploring the woods—not just on the
sense of sight!

We paused to listen to the grating of the cicadas, the
steady knocking of a pileated woodpecker, and the
muffled thump of branches falling to the forest floor.
We inhaled the musky aroma of decaying vegetation and
ran our fingers along the razor-sharp branches of the saw
palmettos.

We left the hammock trail and found the beginning of
the thirteen-mile hiking trail. The main path is marked
by white rectangular blazes painted at eye level on trees.
Cross trails are marked with blue blazes. Two blazes
indicate a change in direction. There is virtually no
danger of getting lost. Without the trail, however, the
hike would be nearly impossible.

After ten or fifteen minutes, we suddenly emerged
from the shady hammock, where the trail is damp and
spongy, to a higher area filled with fragrant pines.

Blue-jays chirped and fussed in the longleaf pines,
and gray squirrels darted across the path, which was
carpeted with pine needles. There was a slight chill in
the air, though the sun shone warmly on our faces as we
wound through green seas of palmettos, and the china-
colored blue sky was visible through the pine branches.
I pointed to deer moss, ferns, sand pine, sabel palms,
bamboo, needle palm, and other flora with which my
friend was unfamiliar. Soon, however, the need for
conversation diminished as we were drawn into the
beauty of the woods.

Beauty in Florida's forests is a subtle matter. The
landscape is not dramatic, and for the uninitiated it may

seem flat and unremarkable. One must walk slowly and pay attention to detail to appreciate it.

While hiking, we stopped, got down on all fours, and examined minute flowers, such as "Innocence"—a white, star-shaped wildflower with a blossom the size of a thumbtack. There were scores of flowers in bloom in the forest. I pointed out wild roses with large, creamy petals. These roses grew in islands of lush subtropical vegetation within the mostly pine forest. My friend was astonished by the richness of life around us.

We walked for over two hours through the scrub, noticing how even slight changes in elevation resulted in changes in the plants that grew around us. Suddenly, three whitetail deer broke through the underbrush and bolted across the trail, their white flags bouncing through the green brush. To see three deer jump across the trail and know we were within a few miles of the Altamonte Mall made us aware of how much is at stake in the battle over the preservation of the Wekiwa River Basin.

I stopped my friend on the trail and made her point out all of the different shades of green she could see. "How then," I asked, "can we call anything 'green' and expect it to refer to one color?" There are thousands of greens in the scrub.

In another hour we came to a marshy bog in a large open space in the forest. These bogs are places where ground water has risen to the surface and loblolly bay trees grow thickly. This is the favored habitat of the rare Florida black bear which can be seen occasionally in Wekiwa park. We circumnavigated the bog. A great blue heron rose up out of the reeds, languidly flapping its powerful wings while its stick legs trailed behind. As we skirted the edge of the clearing, my friend suddenly shouted from across the bog, "Look at this!"

She had found a small green plant with bright red stamen-like protrusions that seemed to be covered with fine, red hair. "These are carnivorous plants," she announced confidently. "Meat-eating plants." She readily identified them as members of the Sundew family. Now I was astonished. "How can you tell?" We got down on our knees for a closer look at the tiny plants. "You see, these are actually glands on the leaves and they secrete a sticky mucus," she explained. "When an insect falls into the plant, the leaves fold over and digest it."

Indeed, one of the plants held a captive fly in its red hairs. I had lived in the area all of my life and had walked the trail many times, but it took an "outsider" to point out to me a rare plant of the forest that I had never noticed.

The day ended with a feeling of deep satisfaction. We started hiking back to the spring in silence. I reflected on what we had learned that day. We had set out in the morning with no particular goal and had ended the day with a delightful discovery of a rare meat-eating plant. I kept thinking that it's a wonder the way a fresh outlook or an outside opinion can open your eyes to something you may think you know so much about. It seemed to me that "natives" and "newcomers" had a lot to learn, if only they would listen to each other.

TURTLE
WATCH

A sliver of moon gives off a faint light and a cool breeze blows in from the Atlantic as I make my way down the beach. Tiny phosphorescent plants that emit a green glow sparkle on the wet sand. I am with a group of about twenty people following park ranger Elizabeth Dupree along the shores of Canaveral National Seashore ten miles south of New Smyrna Beach. It is eleven at night. We are on our way to witness an event that has been taking place on this beach for the past 150 million years.

It has taken me nearly a year to get reservations for the turtle watch, the most popular of the educational programs offered by the park rangers at Canaveral National Seashore. An interesting mix of people—retirees, nature lovers, and a few tourists—have gathered at the Visitor Information Center. We are united by the desire to watch a sea turtle lay her eggs.

Canaveral National Seashore's twenty-four miles of pristine beach provides habitat for nineteen different threatened or endangered species, including three species of sea turtles. Last year rangers found more than 2,000 turtle nests on Canaveral National Seashore. From these nests an estimated 70,000 hatchlings were born.

At the visitor center, Elizabeth Dupree briefs us. "Before we go on our journey," she begins, "I would like everyone to know a little bit about the sea turtles. There are eight different species of sea turtles in the world. Five of these can be found in the coastal waters of Florida." Those species found in Florida are the ridley, hawksbill, green turtle, loggerhead, and the leatherback sea turtle. The leatherback is the largest of the sea turtles and can weigh close to 1,500 pounds. It sometimes nests at Canaveral National Seashore.

While Elizabeth tells us about sea turtles, Bill Bruce, a volunteer, patrols the beach on a three-wheeled cycle looking for nesting turtles. If he finds one, he will radio back to the visitor center, and we will go out to watch the mother turtle lay her eggs.

But Elizabeth warns us to be patient. "It is still unusual to see a turtle. Sea turtles are air-breathing reptiles and they spend most of their lives in the sea," she explains. "They only come to shore to nest and lay their eggs."

We learn that most of the nests at Canaveral National Seashore are made by loggerhead turtles. These turtles eat shellfish, sponges, jellyfish, and other varieties of fish. The turtles mate offshore, where the female remains until conditions are right for nesting. Then she comes ashore after dark to lay her eggs.

We are told of the hazards facing sea turtles, including oil spills, commercial fisherman, and pollution in the ocean. "Developed beaches present all kinds of problems for sea turtles," says Elizabeth Dupree. "Female sea turtles are very intuitive, and they know when an environment is conducive for a nest or not. Beaches with retaining walls and stone embankments do not provide a natural beach for nesting."

She tells of an area north of the park where false crawls have been found. The mother sea turtle has come up to the beach to lay, but encounters a stone embankment. She then retraces her path and returns to the sea, unable to lay.

After a slide show and a video on sea turtles, we chat with the ranger and wait for a chance to go see the turtles. But there is no call from Bill Bruce, and I begin to get discouraged. If no turtle is spotted by eleven o'cock, the turtle watch will be called off. It is no consolation to me that the turtle watch on Sunday night located three laying loggerhead turtles.

I glance at my watch impatiently. It is almost eleven. Then I hear the ranger's radio crackle on her hip. Bill Bruce has located a nesting turtle.

We follow the ranger in our cars down A1A and park about half a mile from where the turtle is believed to be nesting. The night is dark and the sand barks under our feet as we hurry along the beach like some cult on the way to a bizarre ritual.

"Sometimes the nesting process will take up to two hours," Elizabeth Dupree reminds us. "Bright lights or loud noises will alert her to the fact that this isn't a good place to nest. So we need to be quiet and not use our flashlights."

After a twenty-minute walk, we stop as the ranger scouts ahead looking for the turtle. Then, with her flashlight, she signals for us to follow.

When we catch up to her, she is standing beside a nearly 250-pound female loggerhead sea turtle. We make a circle around the turtle, and all of us, young and old alike, are struck speechless by the rare beauty of the moment.

The turtle has crawled beyond the high tide line to the base of the dunes. The higher on the beach she locates her nest, we are told, the less chance that storms will drown the nest with sea water. How she can tell where the high tide line occurs is a mystery.

She has dug a body cavity and lowered her entire body into the sand. With her hind flippers she has made a hole about twelve inches deep for her eggs.

The turtle has just finished laying, the ranger explains, and is now covering the eggs. We watch her work her flippers back and forth, piling sand on the eggs the way a child might bury a toy in the dunes.

"The eggs are about the size of ping-pong balls," says the ranger. "One female will come ashore to nest several times during the season, depositing anywhere from 100 to 160 eggs into each nest."

We remain quiet as we watch the turtle methodically cover her nest. After she is finished, she begins to fill in the body cavity. Although each turtle does it differently, this one pivots in a clockwise direction, filling in the cavity with her flippers and moving the sand around to camouflage the nest.

It will take about sixty days for the eggs to hatch, depending on the temperature of the sand, which affects the length of incubation. The baby turtles usually emerge from the nest at night, when they are less likely to be victims of predators. These turtles are born with the instinct to move toward bright areas. At night the ocean appears brighter than the beach, and this is what makes them return to the sea. If there are bright lights in the area, such as street or building lights, these attract the baby sea turtles and cause them to move toward the light and away from the ocean. As a result, they die. Usually only one in a thousand makes it to maturity, and it takes about twenty years before they are old enough to start mating.

I have heard that the mother sea turtle cries as she lays her eggs. The ranger confirms that tears do flow from the turtle's eyes as she lays. I wonder if she cries for the fate of her babies, whose chances of survival are limited by the many dangers man has put in the way. But the ranger tells us that it is due to sand getting in the turtle's eyes as she lays.

After about an hour, the turtle has finished covering

her nest, and we step back as she turns toward the sea. She moves slowly in the direction of the water and we follow her at a distance. Occasionally, she stops and rests for a moment. She looks around to get her bearings, then continues. In a few weeks this turtle will return to lay a second batch of eggs. But she will never return to this nest.

Soon she reaches the water's edge. I feel a sense of euphoria as we see her struggle into the surf. For a moment her shell glitters in the darkness as a speck of the phosphorescent plant flickers on her back. With her flippers she paddles into the ocean. Slowly, she disappears beneath the waves.

I stand on the beach as if in the wake of a miracle or a dream. I almost doubt what I have seen. But then I watch Bill Bruce and Elizabeth Dupree place a screen over the nest to protect the eggs from raccoons and other creatures. They drive a wooden stake into the sand beside the nest and label it with the date and species of turtle.

I look out to sea, wondering what will become of the mother turtle. Buried in the sand beside me is the future generation of the loggerhead sea turtle. I feel privileged to have experienced this rare, intimate moment in nature, and my eyes become misty. But I'm sure it's just sand getting into them.

PANTHER!

*T*here is one Florida Thanksgiving that I am not going to forget for some time. It proved once again that things in Florida are not always as they seem. This is particularly true of the outdoors. What you see as an unsightly patch of scrub along the roadside might be the habitat of a surprising array of wildlife, some of which are unique to Florida. What appears to be a semi-rural or even suburban area might harbor the last of a vanishing species of animal.

A couple of years ago I saw at Thanksgiving one of the rarest sights of the Florida outdoors, something for which we can all be thankful.

The weather was wet and windy that day. A tropical depression had developed over Nassau, Bahamas, and was blowing fifty-mile-per-hour winds and fifteen-foot seas along the east coast of Florida.

But the rain had stopped in most of Lake County and there was a humid chill in the air. It was about three in the afternoon. My brother and I were heading for a Thanksgiving gathering at our family home on a lake in the country north of Mt. Dora. Suddenly, a large cat weighing at least 100 pounds loped across the road about twenty yards in front of the car. I was driving and I had a long look at the animal. It was tawny-colored and flecked with white on its neck and shoulders. A long tail extended out beyond its rear feet. It was this last feature, the long tail, that made me yell at the same instant my brother Tom yelled, "PANTHER!"

Tom and I were born and raised on the ten acres of orange grove surrounding our parents' home and had both seen many bobcats in the woods and groves near the house. Unlike the bobcat, which is smaller and has a blunt tail, this cat was large and had a tail that nearly dragged the ground.

I stopped the car, and Tom and I returned to the spot of the sighting and searched for tracks. By a stroke of luck, conditions were ideal for tracking. On the side of the road where the panther had crossed, there were patches of exposed sand, still damp from the recent rains.

We stood where we remembered seeing the cat enter the scrubby underbrush and walked in opposite directions, combing the ground for a clue. It did not seem a likely place for a Florida panther. The area is rural, but there are homes spread throughout the orange groves and patches of woods. Perhaps the Ocala National Forest, ten miles farther north, would have been a more logical place to have spotted the cat.

Suddenly, Tom yelled.

When I reached him he was pointing to three clear cat tracks—the biggest I have ever seen.

I had recently read that a man named Bob Stevens of Daytona Beach had made plaster of Paris casts of the tracks of a panther he had sighted in neighboring Volusia County. We resolved to do the same.

Plaster of Paris is not an item I normally carry in my car. We drove to a hardware store, bought a carton of the plaster, stopped at a convenience store, and filled a jug with water. Then we returned to the site, where we prepared the solution.

We poured the plaster of Paris into the tracks. What was supposed to take ten to thirty minutes to dry took well over an hour due to the damp weather. But when we lifted them, they were beautiful impressions.

You hear a lot of talk these days about the endangered Florida panther. Of all the rare species of animals in the Florida wilderness, perhaps the panther is the most elusive. As a result, an almost mystical aura has grown up around this great cat, which once roamed freely in Florida.

The Florida panther is a wide-ranging animal. Scientific tracking by wildlife experts indicates that some panthers range over a 200-square-mile area to find enough to eat. Today, little suitable habitat is left for this magnificent cat.

But all of this was far from my mind that Thanksgiving. We talked excitedly about this rare encounter as we drove to the house. At Thanksgiving dinner, we had a lively exchange as my older brothers told stories of the wildlife they had seen before in the area. But Tom and I knew that none of them could top our sighting of the Florida panther, and we talked glibly of the celebrity our rare encounter might bring us.

After dinner, we packed the plaster casts and mailed them, with a letter detailing the circumstances of our sighting, to the Florida Game and Fresh Water Fish Commission office in Ocala.

Although we needed no further proof ourselves of what we had seen, we felt it was important to make the sighting of the panther official. Experts believe that there are only twenty to fifty panthers left in Florida. The majority are said to inhabit the Everglades. This sighting in Central Florida was significant in that it indicated that the domain of the panther was wider than commonly believed.

Some weeks later, we received a notice on official letterhead from the game & fish commission. The tracks, it stated, were those of a bobcat.

Impossible!

We had seen a cat weighing at least 100 pounds. Bobcats rarely reach forty pounds. The cat we saw had a long tail trailing behind it. Bobcats have blunt "bobbed" tails. I don't know what criteria are used to verify sightings. I don't know who had evaluated the tracks or whether that person would know a panther from a bobcat if he saw one. What we saw was a panther!

The mating season of the Florida panther begins in late November. A litter of up to four kittens is born about three months after mating. I speculated that our panther was searching for a mate.

The sighting was important to me because the Florida panther is a living symbol of a way of life that is also on the eve of extinction. As a native Floridian, I, like the panther, am watching the disappearance of a Florida that I thought, naively, would always be there. While forests and wetlands give way to houses and shopping centers, species such as the Florida panther search desperately for their roles in this changing environment.

I know that I have seen in Central Florida one of the last of Florida's panthers. I hope that this panther survived, found its mate, and produced offspring that will be able to roam freely in the wilderness areas of Florida.

I wish this for the panther and for all Floridians.

GATOR JUNGLE

*I*t's April and you feel restless. Saturday is finally here. You need to get away, but not too far away. The kids are making noises about Disney World or Wet N' Wild. Your wife is looking for something cultural, elevating. You feel trapped. What to do? A drive in the country, out of the noise and traffic and away from the glare of neon, sounds good. But you're too tired to drive very far. You load the kids in the car and drive east on State Road 50, still not sure where you're going. It has to be somewhere outdoors that reminds you that you're not up north anymore. You're in the subtropics, in Florida. You'll have to convince your wife that it's a cultural activity.

"Where are we going, Daddy?" your youngest, the over-inquisitive one, asks.

You turn around and tell her: "We're going to a farm."

"A farm," she whines. "That sounds boring."

Where are you going to find a farm on East 50 anyway? All you see as you drive are 7-Elevens and swaths of bulldozed swamp where shopping centers are under construction.

"An alligator farm," you add in a moment of inspiration. You've heard about Gator Jungle, seventeen miles east of Orlando and six miles west of Titusville. You feel mysteriously drawn there, like it's your karma to take your family to an alligator farm in Christmas, Florida.

"Is this an April Fools' joke?" your wife asks. "Cause April Fools' Day is over."

You pass over the Econlockhatchee River. The landscape is unrelentingly flat, dominated by pastures and stands of pine trees studded with towering cabbage palms. A wooden sign on a pine tree says: "Child Care." There's a telephone number on it. You ask yourself, "Who would leave a child with someone who has tacked her phone number to a dead pine tree on the outskirts of Bithlo?"

You glance back at your youngest, pouting in the back seat. You reach for a pen to write the telephone number down, but you've already whizzed past. You pass J&B's Used Auto Parts, a glorified junkyard, and Brenda's Red Door Saloon: "The friendliest bar in downtown Bithlo." You didn't even realize you were in downtown Bithlo.

You've left civilization, as you know it, behind. "For sale" signs are everywhere. It seems that every square inch of real estate is up for grabs. There is an odd beauty to the landscape that reminds you of some parts of Africa, except for the gigantic microwave dish glittering in front of a dilapidated trailer. You are driving into the exotic heart of the real Florida.

Then you see a billboard: "New Jungle Cruise. Gator Jungle," it announces boldly. "Four thousand gators in their natural habitat." The kids are getting excited. Four thousand gators!

You've never been to a gator farm and you're not sure what to expect. You consider turning back. Something about four thousand gators is unsettling, intimidating. Are they in cages, behind bars? Can they get to you?

The tension is building. Somehow this quest, this journey to Gator Jungle has become the most important thing you have done in your entire life. You're obsessed by it now. You're beginning to wonder if maybe you passed the alligator farm. Then, sprawled along the left-hand side of the road, you see an enormous alligator, its jaws open, its huge white teeth gleaming in the afternoon sun. It's an architectural wonder—a building in the shape of an alligator. You turn into the driveway, still unsure of what you're doing. The sign out front now says there are more than 10,000 gators. You've picked up an additional 6,000 gators in less than a dozen miles.

You enter the gator through a door in its side. The foyer is a gift shop with all kinds of gator regalia: gator jewelry, gator rings, gator belt buckles, gator back scratchers. You have to admit, it's impressive. You shell out seven bucks (four each for kids) for admission into the park. Adam, the guy at the cash register, puts it into perspective for you. "The main business out here," he says, "is raising alligators for the meat and for the hides."

A sign above the cash register reads: "Gator Meat $7.50 lb." Most of the meat goes to restaurants, you're told. On the counter are recipes for "beer fried gator tail" and "broiled gator."

"What do you do with the hides?" you ask.

"We export them to Paris."

You leave the gift shop enlightened. Somehow you thought of it as a farm in name only. But, like a dairy or hog farm, this is agribusiness. You walk over a covered bridge that spans a canal about thirty feet wide. The setting is surprisingly beautiful. Graceful palms grow along the shores. The park is shady and peacocks roost in the oak trees and strut about the property trailing their colorful tail feathers. But along the banks of the canal, in the ooze, half submerged in the water, under trees, in the shade, in the sun—everywhere you look—are thousands of the biggest alligators you have ever seen or imagined in your life. One gator lies absolutely still, half out of the water, its enormous shoulders on the muddy bank, its tail resting in the muck. You have never seen a creature that looked so primordial, so prehistoric. You would not even know he's alive except for the almost imperceptible movement of his belly as he breathes. One of the workers tells you the gator is more than fourteen feet long and weighs 1,000 pounds. He looks up lethargically, and you and your family all step back away from the guard rail in unison. Your wife emits a breathless little noise. Your children stare, silent for the first time since the adventure began. You are awe-struck, humbled.

A sign overhead reads: "Do not tease or molest animals." Who in their right mind, you ask yourself, would tease or molest a 1,000-pound alligator? You feel somehow that you have stumbled onto another continent where the rules are very different.

A petite, dark-haired girl with dark eyes tells you that the boat is leaving soon from the dock. Would you like to come along? The kids race off ahead of you, enthusiastic. Your wife looks at you, shrugs, and you follow the guide.

"What do you feed the gators?" you ask.

"Horse meat."

You board the boat with a couple of other tourists and the girl pushes off from the dock. You squeeze your wife's hand and pull your son and daughter to you. You are now in the middle of the channel, in a boat captained by an adolescent, and you are surrounded by 10,000 alligators, some weighing up to half a ton.

You see one gator with part of its tail missing. "What happened to the gator's tail?" you ask nervously.

"Fights," your guide answers.

"Over on your left," she points out, "is where the

alligator farm is located. Those tanks you see are heated to ninety degrees year around. Right now in those tanks we have thirty to fifty babies in each of them. We have a total of ten thousand gators on the farm."

She points ahead into the swamp. "We have six hundred gators living out here on twenty acres. They range from thirty to eighty years old. These are all breeders for the farm. They lay eggs for us once a year in the month of June. We collect the eggs, take them to the incubators and incubate the eggs. Eggs take two months to hatch. We use the babies for slaughtering."

You are sobered by the reality of the business. It sounds brutal. But it is no different than chicken farming, beef cattle farming, or any other kind of farming for meat.

It doesn't occur to you until later to ask how they collect the eggs. You can hardly believe what the guy inside tells you. "We come out in pairs and one guy holds off the mother with a big stick while the other guy digs out the eggs." In a masterful stroke of understatement he adds, "The mothers are very protective of their nests."

"What is the nest like?"

"It's usually about a two-foot mound of vegetation. It's the rotting vegetation that incubates the eggs, so it's kind of like a compost heap. The mother digs out a hole, puts the eggs in, and keeps piling up the vegetation."

"How long do alligators live?"

"About a hundred twenty years."

A gator bumps against the boat, shaking it. Everywhere you look there are alligators. You are beginning to have serious doubts about having brought your family here. A sign nailed to a tree along the shore is not reassuring. "Bring us more tourists," it reads, "the last ones were delicious." You see more grim alligator farm humor just around the bend: "No trespassing. Violators will be eaten."

On your way out, you ask a few more questions. The staff is friendly, helpful. You are told that the farm has been in operation about twenty-five years and was started by a man named Herman Brooks.

You leave Gator Jungle satisfied. It's been a rewarding and educational adventure. Your children look up to you with admiration. Even your wife seems to have enjoyed it. But as you turn onto State Road 50 and head back to civilization, she asks: "Next weekend, can we go to the symphony?"

JUNIPER
SPRINGS RUN

*T*he Florida my older brother, Martin, remembers was largely rural, a place where a boy could swim and fish in unspoiled water, hike through forests teeming with game, and sit out on the porch on an evening in spring and smell the perfume of orange blossoms blowing in from the groves. He is one of the generation of Floridians who left the state for opportunities elsewhere.

He flew in from California this week for a vacation. Each time he comes home he remarks on the changes in Florida, so I try to take him to places that have remained relatively unchanged. This time we decided to canoe Juniper Springs Run in the Ocala National Forest. This creek begins at the Juniper Springs Recreation area, twenty-two miles east of Silver Springs, and ends at Lake George. The recreation area at Juniper Springs was built in the 1930's by the Civilian Conservation Corps and is one of the oldest national forest recreation areas in the East. The subtropical vegetation there can be found in no other national forest in the continental United States. It is a wonderful area for camping, picnicking, swimming, and hiking.

The park opens at 8 a.m. and we arrived soon after

that. Since the canoe concession does not open until nine o'clock, we walked around the spring. The 20 million gallons of water that bubble up daily from Fern Hammock and Juniper Springs is seventy-two degrees year-round. A few families had already spread blankets out on the grassy area near the main spring, and children swam in the blue-green water.

"Things have not changed that much," my brother remarked as he pointed out the old mill house and paddle wheel that still turned at the head of the spring. We rented a canoe for the day. The fee included transportation back to the spring at the end of the trip. Normally, one would have to have a car or truck waiting at the bridge near the end of the run. But the concession sends a van down every half-hour beginning at one-thirty to pick up the canoes and passengers.

The concession was a short distance from the canoe launch area. By the time we had our canoe in the water and our gear loaded, it was already nine-thirty. We stepped carefully into our canoe. No rafts, floats, or inner tubes are allowed in the creek, and wading is prohibited to protect the fragile ecosystem of the river. A sign near the launch area stated: "This wilderness area is remote and access is limited....Travel at your own risk." Ours would be a one-way trip downstream for seven miles to where Juniper Run passes under the bridge of State Road 19. It would take at least four hours, we calculated, and we were anxious to get started.

We pushed off from the wooden dock and entered another world. The creek was narrow, about ten feet wide, with clear water and a bright, sandy bottom. Birds chirped and screeched at us from the branches of oaks that hung over the water, and palm trees, tangled with vines, grew along the shore. The water was lower than the last time I had paddled downstream. A marker showed a depth of merely one foot ten inches in one place, though it did deepen in others.

For the first half of the trip, the creek remained
narrow, winding, and the vegetation thick, so that we
were shaded from the sun. Wild grape vines curled down
over the water, and we ducked under palm trees that
grew across the creek. Halfway down the stream we
reached a landing with a wooden dock and a picnic table,
where we enjoyed our sandwiches and cold drinks. A
deer came down for a drink, and we watched a family of
otters play near the bank.

After lunch, we headed downstream again. Mullet
and bass swam past us in the transparent water. Beyond
the halfway-point landing, the terrain began to change.
The creek widened and we entered a large open area with
cattails and saw grass. The sun burst through the vegetation, illuminating turtles that sunned on the sandy banks,
and the blue sky shone against the shoreline of green
pine trees.

Martin talked about the old days as we floated past
hundred-year-old cypresses, their cone-like "knees" jut-
ting up out of the water. In fact, it was as though we were
going back in time, or as if the hands of the clock were
slowly reversing. All the intervening years of school,
work, marriage, children, and adult responsibilities re-
ceded, and we were children again. Life was as simple
as an afternoon dip in a cold spring on a summer day. We
lifted our paddles from the water and drifted with the
current as time stood still, as motionless as a yellow
butterfly asleep on a banana leaf.

The air was musty with the rich decay of the subtropics and our faces tingled from the sun. A great blue
heron picked its way gingerly through the lily pads and
an alligator, sunning on the bank, slipped into the water
in front of our canoe. We drifted silently for hours in
this time warp, no longer men with offices and telephones, requisitions to sign and appointment calendars,
but boys traveling back through time, across the years
that separated us from the mystery of childhood and the

enchantment of nature in its most unspoiled state.

The distant drone of the highway awakened us from our daydreams. It was nearly two o'clock. We had been on the river more than four hours as we approached the two-lane bridge where State Road 19 arches over the creek. We beached our canoe at Juniper Wayside Park and waited for the van that would bring us back to Juniper Springs Recreation Area. As we pulled our canoe onto the sandy shore, a couple wading in the shallow creek called out, "How was it?"

Neither of us answered, as if talking about the trip might somehow break the spell. But finally my brother said, "Nice," and put his hand on my shoulder. "Real nice."

WINTER
IN FLORIDA

*T*he first day of winter falls on December 21 this year. This is the winter solstice, when in the northern hemisphere the sun is farthest south of the equator. This is also the holiday season.

The holidays mean something different to each of us. I asked my wife, Wren (an opera singer raised in Louisville, Kentucky) what this time of year meant to her.

"Handel's *Messiah*," she said. This came as no surprise. My wife was named for the wren which is said to have the loveliest song of any bird in North America. My Wren has the loveliest soprano voice of any woman in North America—at least in my opinion. "And snow," she added. "We always hoped that we would have snow on Christmas day."

I'm a rare bird myself: a native Floridian in a state where most of the population was born elsewhere. I was raised on an orange grove a mere five degrees above the Tropic of Cancer. Snow is not the first thing I think of when winter is mentioned. In fact, the first time I saw snow I was twenty-one years old, passing on a Greyhound bus through the Sangre de Cristo Mountains in northern New Mexico.

On that distant winter afternoon when I first saw

snow, I had waited anxiously all morning for it to fall. I thought that it would mark a kind of beginning for me and that I was on the brink of a new life. A constellation of new and exciting experiences waited to touch my life. I imagined that the multi-faceted flakes that began to fall that afternoon in New Mexico would cover the flat and swampy subtropical landscape of my childhood.

As it began to snow, the laconic Navahos on the bus with me turned their brown faces to the windows and then back again, unimpressed, while I stared out in amazement at the whitening countryside.

I turned to the old man in the seat next to me and announced, "It's snowing!" But he kept staring straight ahead at the back of the seat in front of him. I wanted to get up and shout, "Look, everyone, look, it's snowing."

I thought of going up to the driver and asking him to stop so that I could get out and feel the snow, make snowballs, build a snowman. But then I realized how foolish it would seem. I kept quiet so as not to reveal my inexperience. It was a difficult secret to keep because the snow kept falling all the way to Flagstaff.

Later, after I survived several winters in Iowa, my first snowstorm in Arizona paled in comparison. One Christmas season in Iowa the wind-chill factor was sixty-five degrees below zero and not a car on my block could start. I sat in my room, looking out the window at the ten-foot snow drifts and stranded cars, and asked myself, "How can people live like this?"

It took some adjustment for this Florida boy. I learned that it required gloves, hat, scarf, boots, and a very warm coat. The coat I had brought from Florida was the heaviest lined coat I could find. When I put it on, it seemed like an absurdly weighty thing to have to wear around all the time. However, the first cold day in Iowa, the wind cut through it like it was paper. I soon realized it was not nearly heavy enough. I put it away and bought a good down jacket and wool hat.

Now that I am back in Florida, it seems hard to believe that I ever experienced such weather. Northerners nostalgic for their home always tell me that the only time they ever miss snow is during the holiday season. But the holidays can be beautiful no matter where you are. Florida is no exception.

My wife says she thinks of winter as a time for sledding. But when I think of winter, I think of the harvesting of oranges. In December the early fruit—navels, parson brown, hamlin, and pineapple oranges, to name a few varieties—is harvested. Despite all the mechanization of industry in Florida, this job is still done by hand. The groves are filled with crews of pickers who scale ladders and fill their bags with oranges. The air smells of crushed orange peels and wood smoke as workers huddle around small fires in the groves.

I feel more energetic in the winter. The air is chilled and I am moved to get outdoors. I like hiking in the forest. But one must be cautious because winter also marks the beginning of hunting season. Hundreds of hunters take to the woods in pursuit of the white-tailed deer.

In Greek and Roman mythology, Orion was the hunter whom Diana loved. She killed him accidentally and placed him in the heavens as a constellation. Winter nights in Florida are clear and crisp. The stars twinkle in the sky like cold points of light. This is the season when Orion is prominent in the southern sky in the early evening. The constellation is high off the horizon and the bright stars, Rigel and Betelgeuse, glitter in the inky night.

Winter in Florida is also the season when large numbers of migratory birds arrive from the North. Every year a host of ducks—canvasback, teal, merganser, and pintail—fly into the lake in front of our home. Last year, a flock of Canada geese arrived on their annual migration south. Because we had an unusually warm winter, they stayed on throughout the season, and I watched the graceful birds from my living room with a pair of binoculars.

Florida can even boast its own town named Christmas. Approximately twenty-three miles east of downtown Orlando on State Road 50 is the town of Christmas, Florida, with an estimated population of 4,000. Normally, the post office at Christmas processes 700 to 800 pieces of mail a day. However, each year during the holiday season some 25,000 cards, letters, and parcels arrive daily at the tiny Christmas Post Office so that they can be stamped with the unusual postmark: Christmas, Florida.

But not all Florida winters bring happy memories. I shall never forget Christmas morning of 1983 and January of 1985 when killer back-to-back freezes changed the face of Florida forever. Perhaps those were the most bitter winters of all. We watched in '83 as the mercury dropped and my parents' satsuma grove, where I had spent many years working and playing, was killed. Thousands of acres of Florida's citrus trees were wiped out in a single night. Many of the groves that survived the freeze of '83 succumbed to the cold in '85, and a traditional way of life that had sustained so many people for so long was, as they say, gone with the wind.

Newcomers say there is no change of season in Florida. Of course, they soon realize that this is a misconception. But some people who have been here long enough to consider themselves Floridians tell me they can hardly detect the change of seasons since it is so subtle. One season, they say, seems to slip unnoticed into the next.

For me, the change is abrupt and noticeable, though it is difficult to explain to others. There is a feeling in fall, maybe it's a change in the air, a smell, perhaps something in the song of the mourning dove or the way the bobwhite whistles. I can't say exactly. But I wake up one morning and I know winter is at hand. After a long summer, most of us are glad it is on the way.

The images of Christmas to which many of us have become accustomed are the tall fir tree decorated with icicles and a countryside blanketed with snow. If Florida seems an unlikely setting for the holiday season, think of the Christ child born in a stable in Bethlehem. It's likely that the stable stood in a grove of date palms and that a warm breeze blew across the desert on that holy night.

ISLAND
OF THE
OWL CLAN

A totem in the shape of an owl was discovered in 1955 near Hontoon Island in the St. Johns River west of DeLand. This totem, now in the Florida State Museum in Gainesville, is the largest artifact of ancient native American culture found in Florida. Who carved this totem? When was it carved? What tribe did it represent? I went to Hontoon Island to find the answer to these questions and to see the Indian shell mound there.

Hontoon Island State Park is located approximately twelve miles west of Interstate 4 in DeLand. The island can be reached by private boat or by a ferry operated free of charge by the State Park Service. The ferry runs hourly during the week and on demand (sound your horn) on weekends and holidays.

I parked my car in the small parking area on the mainland. The shore of the island, no more than one hundred yards across the river, was lined with palm trees and people fishing with cane poles from its bank.

"I understand there is a shell mound on the island," I said to the ranger as I climbed aboard the ferry with three or four other people carrying fishing poles and bait buckets.

"That's right. Are you an archaeologist?"

"No," I laughed and introduced myself. "I'm a writer. I'm interested in the totem that was found on this island and I'd like to see the shell mound."

The ranger directed me to the nature trail that leads to the shell mound. I strolled across the shady picnic area overlooking the St. Johns River and came to an observation tower. I climbed the metal steps of the eighty-foot tower.

Looking out over the 1,650-acre island, I could easily imagine what it had been like when the Timucuan Indians lived here. According to experts, small nomadic bands of Indians entered Florida more than 14,000 years ago. These early settlers later split into various groups that evolved their own cultures based on the natural environment where they settled. When Juan Ponce de Leon came to Florida in 1513, numerous tribes, including the Apalachee, Calusa, Tequesta and the Timucua, lived in Florida. But the Native American population declined rapidly as a result of diseases brought to their land by the Europeans.

There were more than 40,000 Timucuans in central and northeast Florida when the Spanish arrived. These Native Americans lived in log houses made from the trunks of cabbage palms. They hunted the abundant game and fished with hooks made from the bones of deer. They also made bracelets and necklaces from bones and shells. With sharpened bones they sewed together skins to make clothing. When Spain abandoned her colony in 1763, the few remaining Timucuans fled with the Spanish.

Few physical remains of Timucuan culture are unearthed today. However, the most common remnants we have of their existence are the shell mounds which they left. Shell mounds, also called shell middens, are trash heaps of shells that were discarded by the Indians over a period of some 600 years. During the 19th and early

20th centuries, shell mounds in Florida were carelessly leveled to construct roads. Today, these archaeological sites are studied by scientists hoping to learn more about the Timucua. Perhaps the most spectacular shell midden in Florida is Turtle Mound at Canaveral National Seashore near New Smyrna Beach. From a boardwalk that leads to the top of the mound, there is a commanding view of the Atlantic Ocean and the East Coast.

In back of the observation tower on Hontoon Island, I followed a dim trail, thickly overgrown with vines and pale blue flowers, and then a sand road that led to the beginning of the Indian Mound Nature Trail near the camping area. This self-guiding trail winds through a hardwood hammock. It takes about fifty minutes to reach the shell mound.

I followed the trail as it snaked through a dense growth of palms and live oaks. These massive oak trees were once used for shipbuilding. In fact, Hontoon Island served as a boat yard before it was purchased by the state of Florida for preservation in 1967.

I passed through thick patches of saw palmetto. The buds and berries of this plant were eaten by the Timucuans, and they tanned leather with tannic acid extracted from the roots of the plant.

As I made my way along the trail, entranced by the lush forest of slash pine, sweetgum, and southern magnolia, I saw a wild turkey about fifty feet in front of me. I watched the bird through binoculars as it raced off in the thick underbrush. Later, the ranger told me that the island is rich in wildlife. Not only are there wild turkeys, but also deer, wild hogs, and black bear.

A small boardwalk passed over a wet area of the trail through a shady patch of ferns. I read the interpretive sign: "Ferns are one of the oldest groups of living land plants and were most abundant during the formation of coal beds 300 million years ago. Ferns do not produce buds or flowers. They reproduce by spores which appear as rust-colored spots on the underside of the leaf or on separate stems. These spores are very small and can be carried by the wind for many miles."

I came to a small clearing that opened onto the river. Offshore a couple of fishermen were casting their bait into the tea-colored water. After several more minutes, I reached a warning sign erected by the Division of Recreation and Parks: "Florida law prohibits digging or removing artifacts from state property."

The trail rose slightly above the surrounding lowlands and I followed the path up onto the mound itself. The ground beneath my feet glowed from the white snail shells. There were actually two mounds, each about twenty feet high and covered with vegetation. The Timucuan Indians who had once lived in this area ate snails that they gathered from the river. They had piled their discarded shells here for ceremonial purposes. These high mounds also provided refuge from floods during hurricanes.

The trail ended abruptly atop the mound at the foot of a massive live oak. I took a few moments to catch my breath and reflect on the life of the Timucuan people. I could not think of a more rich and beautiful environment in which to live.

I started back on the same trail on which I had come. This trail would bring me back to the ferry and to the Florida of honking horns, traffic jams, and shopping centers. For just a moment, I hesitated. I could live on this island on berries and roots, I thought to myself, and catch fish from the river. I shouldered my pack, knowing that this was just a fantasy. I was thankful at least that the state of Florida had preserved Hontoon Island for camping, fishing, and picnicking.

Back at the docks, I found the replica of the owl totem that stands in the picnic area. "About 600 years ago," the sign near the totem stated, "the Indians who lived here cut a large pine tree and, using a shell ax and shark-toothed knife, fashioned this totem which was erected near the river so that all who passed would know that this was the village of the owl clan."

I saw the ferry prepare to take another load of passengers to the mainland. I hastily read the other interpretive sign near the totem. "What was the function of these carvings in Indian life? Each may be a different 'coat of arms' that identified a particular clan or social group. They may have had deeper meaning as part of a ritual, possibly the guardians of a burial site."

In their book, *Florida Archaeology*, Jerald T. Milanich and Charles H. Fairbanks argue: "It is doubtful if the figurine represents a clan totem, like the totem poles found elsewhere in the United States. Since the owl was generally viewed by southeastern aborigines as a symbol of evil or bad luck, the carving may have been placed near a ceremonial area...to keep away persons who were not allowed to deal with sacred paraphernalia."

I jumped aboard the ferry for the return trip to the mainland. As the boat cast off, I looked back over the island. Although I had not solved the mystery of the owl totem that the Indians of Hontoon Island had carved more than 600 years ago, I still felt a strange bond with these people of the owl clan.

THE DISAPPEARING WOODPECKER

I am sitting in my office, sipping a cup of coffee and putting the finishing touches on another "Tropical Son" column, when the phone rings.

"I need some information," a young lady with a silky voice says.

I set down my coffee cup, flip off the monitor on my word processor, and lean back. "What's up?"

She hesitates a moment. When she finally speaks, her voice has an edge to it. "I was wondering," she begins haltingly, "what you can tell me about the red-cockaded woodpecker."

Ah, yes, the old woodpecker routine. "It's a rare bird," I say. "On the list of endangered species. Used to be a lot of them in Florida. Their population has been dwindling due to habitat loss. What else you want to know about them?"

"Everything."

Hey, no problem. I reach over and take down a volume of R.J. Longstreet's *Birds in Florida*, published by Trend House.

"You got a pencil?" I ask.

I hear her rummaging around for a moment. Then she says, "Yes."

"The red-cockaded woodpecker" I read from the book, "is from seven to eight inches in length, has white bars on a black back, white spots on the wings, and white underparts. The cheeks are white and on either side of the black crown there are patches of white. Red feathers on both sides of the crown give the bird a rather jaunty appearance and form a sort of cockade that gives the species its name."

I've never seen a woodpecker like that, I say to myself. I read further. "This friendly woodpecker chooses its mate in January and February, and excavates a home in a living pine from twenty to seventy feet above the ground. Late in April or early May three or four white satiny eggs are laid. The active pair converse in noisy chattering notes as they work and the air resounds with their shrill, clear calls, especially in breeding season."

Now I'm intrigued. Actually, I don't know much at all about this endangered species, and I certainly have never seen one. "Anything else you want to know?" I ask her.

"Yeah. Where can you see one in Central Florida?"

I'm stumped. Where do you find a red-cockaded woodpecker in Central Florida? The question has never come up before. "Tell you what," I say, stalling. "Let me do some legwork, see what I can find out this weekend. I'll get back to you on Monday."

I put the phone down and go to the window. A stiff breeze is blowing across the lake and a couple of blue jays are hassling a squirrel. Why is this woman so interested in woodpeckers? I ask myself. I'm a writer, not a private detective. But her phone call has put me on the trail of the nearly extinct red-cockaded woodpecker.

I call Charlie Matthews, the park manager of Tosohatchee State Reserve, east of Orlando. "I'm looking for a woodpecker," I tell him.

"Oh, yeah?" he says.

"Have you seen any red-cockaded woodpeckers out there?"

Charlie is no more surprised by my question than if I'd asked if he had any trees out there. "We know of one nest, " he says. "But there has been no activity around it by birds in several years."

"That so?" I say, taking notes.

"Now the year before last," he adds, "it was obvious that the nest cavity had been cleaned up some. But none of us ever saw a bird. What happened, we don't know. One thing we did do within the last year is more specifically manage the area around that tree. Hopefully, by getting some of the vegetation down around the tree, it will encourage them to return."

"But there are none out there now?"

"Not that we know of."

Sensing my disappointment, Charlie offers,   "Of course, we have a number of other species that are of vital concern, like the gopher tortoise and the Eastern indigo snake. It's not uncommon to see several of those every day."

"I'm not looking for tortoises," I say roughly. "I'm looking for woodpeckers."

I thank him and hang up.

I call Ralph Costa, a biologist with the National Forest Service in Tallahassee. I'm told he is a leading authority on the bird.

"Do you know of any places in Central Florida where one can see the red-cockaded woodpecker?" I ask.

Ralph doesn't hesitate a second. "The Ocala National Forest has ten or twelve active colonies."

"In what sort of habitat does the woodpecker live?"

"The vast majority of the birds live in mature longleaf pine forests. When Columbus hit the beach, we had probably seventy million acres of that kind of forest. Now, four million acres is all that remains."

"How many red-cockaded woodpeckers would you

estimate are left in Florida?"

Ralph considers the question a moment. "Probably somewhere around two thousand. That represents a fifth or more of the birds left in the world."

I thank him for his help.

Now I'm consumed by the case. I want to find out where to see a red-cockaded woodpecker in Central Florida. The Ocala National Forest is more than 430,000 acres of woods. You don't just go out and expect to find an endangered species.

I call Edith Dill of the Oklawaha Valley Audubon Society. As it turns out, she is leading a field trip to an area of the Ocala National Forest inhabited by several colonies of red-cockaded woodpeckers.

I meet the group at seven-thirty the next morning in Lake County at the Forest Service Work Center on State Road 19 near Lake Dorr. This is at the southern edge of the national forest.

Mitch Cohen, ranger of the Seminole District of the Ocala National Forest, gives us a short orientation to the habits of the red-cockaded woodpecker: "Usually, in a colony there is one mated pair that lays the eggs in the spring and raises the young. The other birds are helpers. They live in the neighboring cavity trees. They are usually the younger birds, the sons of the parent birds. They help maintain the colony and help the adults raise the babies."

We follow the rangers to a remote site off of Forest Road 572 on the east side of Lake Dorr. It is midmorning and the deep woods are fragrant with pine needles. We enter a park-like stand of seventy-to-eighty-year-old longleaf pines. White blazes on their trunks mark the cavity trees of the red-cockaded woodpeckers.

We gather around one of the trees while Ranger Jim Thorsen explains the Forest Service's augmentation program: "Our augmentation program translocates birds to a colony so they can mate and increase the population.

What we're doing is bringing birds from the Apalachicola National Forest in the Panhandle of Florida. We are translocating a female bird to come into these cavities that have only a male bird. Hopefully, they'll join together, be friends, and mate."

He points to a pine with a single, perfectly round hole drilled into it. There are a series of smaller holes drilled around the nest cavity. A large quantity of sap has dripped down the side of the tree like the wax that flows down the shaft of a candle. Jim explains that there is more sap flowing out of the tree than the last time he was here. This indicates that the woodpecker has been active at this tree.

He points to another pine. "We brought a female in here about a year ago and monitored it. Evidently they didn't hit it off. The male stayed and the female went over and nested in a cavity tree over there. We don't know where the female is right now. We think she is somewhere in the woods but we don't know exactly where."

Jim takes a pine branch and scratches on the base of the tree to arouse the woodpecker if he is inside the cavity. But there is nobody home.

Although we haven't seen the woodpecker itself, we have learned a great deal about its habits and its habitat.

"Now that you know where the tree is," the ranger tells us, "you can come out here at about five o'clock in the morning and by daylight you will probably see the bird come out."

Early Monday morning I ring the young lady who put me on to the case of the red-cockaded woodpecker. She sounds sleepy when she answers the phone.

I take a sip of coffee and ask, "What are you doing at five o'clock tomorrow morning?"

BLUE SPRING

"All of a sudden I saw something bob up and down in the river. I thought it was a human head. Then this thing rose out of the water beside the boat. It had huge whiskers and gigantic nostrils. It started to follow our boat."

"What was it?" I asked my wife, impatiently. She was telling me about a fishing trip on the St. Johns River she had taken with her grandfather when she was eight years old.

"Granddaddy called it a sea cow," she said. "I even reached out and touched it on the nose. I'll never forget that day. But when I told people about it later, no one would believe me. So it was a secret that Granddaddy and I shared."

There is something wonderfully mysterious about the endangered manatee, which many old-time Floridians call "sea cows." It is an odd-looking creature, and an unforgettable sight. Early sailors supposedly mistook manatees for mermaids, although I don't see how.

If you want to see a manatee for yourself, February is a good time for it. Blue Spring State Park, about twenty-five miles north of Orlando, is a good place.

I went to Blue Spring to see the manatees. In the

process, I learned that looking for something can be nearly as much fun as finding it. I was thinking about manatees because the weather was getting cool, and I knew that the manatees would be starting their annual migration inland to warmer waters.

In the small town of Orange City, I turned off of U.S. Highway 17-92 onto French Avenue. After about two miles I turned left into the entrance of the state park. Spreading live oaks festooned with Spanish moss cast shadows on the road.

"Are the manatees in yet?" I asked the ranger at the gate.

"There are about four of them here now," he said as he handed me a pamphlet that described the park and featured a picture of a mother manatee, known as a cow, and her baby, known as a calf, on the cover.

As I drove past the gate and into the main area of the park, I realized that Blue Spring State Park is a scenic piece of Old Florida. It was originally the home of the Timucuan Indians who hunted, fished, and gathered snails from the area around the spring some three to four thousand years ago. In the late 1800's, archaeologists unearthed pottery, arrowheads, tools, clay figures, and other remnants of Timucuan culture from the shell mounds at Blue Spring.

Blue Spring has experienced the ebb and flow of Florida's history over the years. The English botanist, John Bartram, explored Blue Spring on January 4, 1766, as the official naturalist of the British Crown.

In the early 19th century, white settlers began to enter the area of the spring and most of the Timucuans were wiped out. Louis Thursby arrived at Blue Spring in 1856 and built a house atop a shell mound in 1872.

A less intrepid explorer, I parked my car near the Thursby home and strolled across the expansive lawn. Guided tours of the restored, three-story house are given Thursday through Sunday from 11 a.m. to 4 p.m.

The Thursbys established a port for steamboats arriving in Blue Spring from the St. Johns River. From here, oranges and other citrus fruits from the surrounding groves were shipped north. A passenger station accommodated Florida's first tourists, who arrived by steamboat at Blue Spring. These tourists included boatloads of hunters who came to hunt alligators, deer, bear, and other wildlife. People seeking respite from ailments through Florida's fabled restorative springs and mineral waters also arrived by boat. Even European nobility came on river tours to the spring.

More than one hundred years after Bartram explored the area, poet Sidney Lanier described Blue Spring in his guide to Florida. In 1885, a handbook published by a Florida railway company to attract settlers and investors to Florida spoke of the "rare beauty of the great Blue Springs." But neither publication mentioned manatees.

I walked past the Thursby home to the edge of Blue Spring run. I saw some old pilings of the original steamboat docks, as well as the rusted shaft of a paddle-wheel from the steamboat "Fannie Dugan" that was abandoned near Blue Spring in the late 1800's.

Although there are no steamboats at Blue Spring today, there is a tour boat, "The John Bartram," from which you can explore the area of the St. Johns River around the spring on a two-hour cruise. Canoes can also be rented at the spring. But I passed up these attractions to search for manatees.

Blue Spring was acquired by the Florida Park Service in 1972, and it serves as a manatee sanctuary and winter refuge for these endangered mammals. There are approximately 1,200 manatees left in the United States, most of them in Florida.

I walked down the boardwalk that leads to the crystalline spring. The water was a phosphorescent aquamarine. These waters are home to freshwater fish such as catfish, striped bass, bullhead, gar, crappie, and some fish that swim upriver from the Atlantic.

I scanned the surface of the water and looked along the palmetto-lined edges of the spring for signs of the manatee.

Because the West Indian manatee is a warmblooded mammal, the water in which it lives must be at least sixty-five degrees Fahrenheit. For most of the year they live in warm coastal waters. About seventy-five manatees are said to inhabit the St. Johns River. But in the winter, around the latter part of November when the water temperature in the river begins to drop, the manatees move into Blue Spring. The water in the spring is seventy-two degrees year-round while the water in the St. Johns can drop to as low as fifty degrees. The manatees can generally be seen from November until March. But I could see no sign of the manatees.

According to park officials, some twenty-four manatees come to Blue Spring each winter. The largest of these weighs nearly a ton and is over ten feet long. Yet they are gentle creatures. For nearly two years, manatees nurse their young with milk from glands located near their flippers.

Manatees eat aquatic plants such as water hyacinths and eel grass and help keep rivers and streams clear of these plants. Some manatees eat up to 200 pounds of plants a day. Since there is little vegetation in the spring itself, I concluded that the manatees must have been out in the river foraging for food where I could not see them.

The manatee's only natural enemy is man, and they are often victims of his carelessness and cruelty. Rangers at Blue Spring say that most of the manatees that come into the spring bear scars from boat propellers. Many others are killed each year by motorboats. It makes me sick to think that this peaceful creature may someday be eradicated by thoughtless people who roar through Florida's rivers and channels in high-speed powerboats with little or no regard for the wildlife around them.

I walked along the boardwalk that skirts Blue Spring

to an area where there are ladders for descending into the spring. I donned my mask and flippers and eased into the pool. The water was bracing to say the least. I dove below the surface. The floor of the spring was sandy white and littered with white shells that looked luminous through the crystal green water. Schools of fish darted just out of reach.

With an eye out for manatees, I swam upstream toward the boil, the source of Blue Spring. The spring pumps about 100 million gallons of water a day into the St. Johns River. It was difficult swimming against the current but I finally reached the boil, a pool of water about thirty yards wide. On the bottom of the pool is the opening of a great shaft that descends straight down for hundreds of feet into the Florida aquifer. The water surging up from the shaft contains little oxygen or food, so few fish are seen around the boil. The water, driven by the pressure below the surface, "boils" up from the shaft and rushes down Blue Spring Run to the St. Johns River.

Divers can enter this underground passage, where two logs form a cross over the entrance to the cavern. The rising current pushes against them as they dive straight down into the passage. At 100 feet below the surface, they reach a round chamber that is said to be full of branches, logs, and fossils as well as railroad spikes and parts of cars. At 120 feet in depth, a huge boulder, known as Cork Rock, partially blocks the shaft. At that depth, the surge of the current boiling up from the aquifer, as well as the intense pressure under water, prevents the divers from passing farther into the cavern. No one has ever reached the actual source of Blue Spring.

Swimming over the entrance to the mysterious source of the spring and inspired by the tranquil beauty around me, I had forgotten, for a moment, why I had come. I had come in search of the manatee. What I found, once again, was the lush, exotic beauty of Florida's outdoors. I lay on my back and floated lazily downstream. I thought back over the events of the day as I watched an osprey circle overhead in the cloudless blue sky. I never did see a manatee. I hope that you will go to Blue Spring between November and March, a period when you are most likely to see one of these elusive creatures. Perhaps you will have better luck than I did. But it really doesn't matter. After all, the search is as rewarding as the find.

THE HURRYING
WORLD

I'm an unusual Floridian. I live on the same ten acres of land where I was born. Our home is in the quiet country of Lake County. The scenic road that winds back to our ranch snakes its way through lush orange groves, along the shores of crystalline lakes, and under the canopy of sprawling oaks drenched with Spanish moss.

A sand road leads back to our house. To the left, a fence-line overgrown with bamboo separates us from the Mediterranean-style chateau on the adjoining property. The home, former headquarters for the Banks family groves, was built by Dr. Edgar James Banks in 1924. It seems an apt residence, with its courtyards and arches, for this archaeologist and explorer who excavated the Babylonian ruin of Bismaya and discovered the oldest statue in the world, of the pre-Babylonian King, David, of 4500 B.C.

Ours is a simpler house that overlooks a still unspoiled lake. The house was designed and built by my father and was once surrounded by our satsuma grove, the most delicious of Florida's citrus fruits. Of course, the freeze of 1983 nearly put an end to the whole "grove culture," as Florida writer Bob Morris calls it. Now our land is in pasture, and the hay is sold to the many horse ranches that are springing up nearby. But I pay for my romantic attachment to the land on which I was born, for I drive well over an hour to work. So, against the backdrop of this tranquility, my wife and I must face the horrors of commuting.

We set our alarm for 5:30 a.m. When it rings (or beeps, as ours does), I reach over, turn it off, and fall back to sleep. Usually I wake back up with a start, look over, and it's six o'clock and still dark outside. I spring from my bed and the race is on. On my way to the bathroom I turn on the stove, crack two eggs into the pan, pour a half cup of grits into boiling water, flip on the coffee-maker, rush to the closet, and pull my clothes for the day off their hangers. In the meantime breakfast is starting to burn. Wren is too busy getting herself ready to bother with breakfast. When I've finished eating, it's 6:15. I run to the shower. Out of the shower I jump into my clothes—socks, socks, where are my socks? Got them! It's 6:30. I slap my pants pocket for my keys, got 'em; my rear end for my wallet, got it; coat pocket for my appointment book, got it. Blast off!

I give Wren a quick kiss as she takes off for work ahead of me. I lock the door behind me and am halfway to the car when I remember that I left the stove on. I fumble with the lock, get inside, switch off the stove, and glance quickly at the clock. It's 6:40. There is no time to lose. I'll have to hit every green light on State Road 436 to get to the University of Central Florida by 8 a.m. when my first class begins.

I put the key in the ignition (crank, baby, crank). Miraculously, it does. I swing onto the road, and a hot-shot in a BMW flies past in excess of seventy miles per hour. Commuting is becoming a way of life even in the country. As if the pace car at Daytona Speedway has just whizzed by, I roar after him in a rush to get to class on time. It's 6:45. In twenty minutes I am on State Road 46 heading toward Sanford. A few minutes later, I turn onto Markham Woods Road. From there it's a straight shot to State Road 439 and I have time, while driving through the pleasant countryside of Seminole County, to reflect on the absurdity of hurtling past pine woods and upscale housing developments in a metal contraption at a dangerously high speed.

Another car flies past me, rounds the corner near Heathrow, and disappears. I glance at my watch: 7:20. I pass Alaqua and catch the red light at State Road 434. I have thirty minutes to get all the way across Orlando. The light changes. I floor it and get up on Interstate 4. The guy who passed me in his BMW forty minutes ago appears beside me. I wonder what good it has done him to drive so fast when this is as far as he's gotten. It's all a matter of catching the lights, I conclude.

We're neck and neck as we get off I-4 at S.R. 436. The light is turning yellow so he accelerates, swings over in front of me, and roars through. I'm caught on red and it's 7:35. When the light turns, I hesitate less than a second, and the bozo behind me is already blasting his horn like he has a plane to catch.

"Give it a rest," I scream into the rear-view mirror.

That is when I know I've finally left the tranquility of my home and am into the savage heart of the urban experience—I'm starting to scream in traffic. I hit two more red lights before I've even gotten past the Altamonte Mall, but then I start catching greens. It's 7:45 and all pretense of courteous driving has been discarded as cars cut in and out of traffic, their horns blaring, jockeying for position. The guy in the BMW is stopped at the light on U.S. Highway 17-92, and as I pull up beside him, he's fuming. I can see his hands tremble as he lights a cigarette. I wonder what job he is rushing to. He's probably a brain surgeon with an operation scheduled for eight o'clock.

We're running even through the light at Howell

Branch Road. At University Boulevard the light is turning yellow, but I push through and I'm on the home stretch. In my rear-view I see the brain surgeon stalled at the light, and I can't keep from gloating. Minutes later I pull into my parking spot in front of the Humanities and Fine Arts building with forty seconds to spare. A short hike across campus and I'm at my desk in front of twenty-five eager freshman. A sense of relief passes over me as I open our literature book and begin the day.

"William Wordsworth," I say to the class, "wrote the following lines in *The Prelude*:

When from our better selves we have too long
Been parted by the hurrying world, and droop,
Sick of its business, of its pleasures tired,
How gracious, how benign, is Solitude."

I look up at the class with a broad smile and ask, "Can anyone tell me what he meant by that?"

A LITTLE BIT
OF HEAVEN

I am seated on an ornately decorated stone bench high above the surrounding subtropics in a garden of lilies, gardenias, and birds-of-paradise. The air is fragrant with the scent of camphor from nearby camphor trees, and the wind carries strains of Camille Saint-Saens' "The Swan" to my ears. Have I died and gone to heaven? I'm not sure.

I'm always a bit skeptical about places that purport to be improvements on nature. I prefer nature in its wild state, unadorned (or unimproved) by people. But I've come to Bok Tower Gardens in Lake Wales to see if it is really, as the brochure promises, "a restful, quiet, beautiful spot."

Bok Tower Gardens is an unusual nature preserve about an hour south of Orlando off U.S. Highway 27 in Lake Wales. The centerpiece of the extensive gardens is a carillon tower. A carillon is an instrument made up of chromatically tuned bells that are sounded by hammers controlled by a keyboard.

Bok Tower Gardens was created on Iron Mountain, which at 295 feet is one of the highest points in Florida. Well before one reaches the entrance of the gardens, the tower can be seen peeking above the horizon. I wind my way through orange groves and between lakes on the climb up to the gardens and arrive at the Singing Tower under a threatening sky—a portentous beginning for an afternoon in paradise.

The Gardens covers 130 acres. The three-dollar admission fee is a pleasant surprise. I expected to shell out the kind of money usually extorted from visitors to Central Florida's attractions. But Bok Tower Gardens is owned by a nonprofit corporation, The American Foundation.

The Gardens was created and endowed in 1923 by an editor and publisher, Edward Bok. This also comes as a surprise, since I have never found editors or publishers to be particularly generous folks.

Edward Bok, a Dutch immigrant, transformed this sandy hill outside of Lake Wales into a sanctuary for wildlife and as a refuge for the human spirit. He followed the example of his grandfather, who turned a desert island in the North Sea into a beautifully landscaped bird sanctuary. The skeptic in me keeps wondering what this hill outside of Lake Wales may have looked like before it was "transformed." But I keep an open mind.

Mr. Bok bought the land in Lake Wales in 1922 and employed a landscape architect, Frederick Law Olmstead Jr., to design the gardens, and architect Milton B. Medary to design the tower.

I walk up the main path through lushly landscaped flower beds. Yellow butterflies light in a bed of pink Brazilian plume bushes. I am surrounded by azaleas and camellias. Throughout the gardens are stands of oaks and pines encircled by ferns and flowering shrubs. Graceful magnolia trees shade beds of monkey grass, and the paths are lined with palms, their trunks covered with fig vines.

Along the walkway are reflecting pools where swans swim placidly. Gazebos and fountains draw the eye to secluded portions of the gardens. A sign along the main path quotes John Burroughs, who wrote of the gardens: "I come here to find myself. It is so easy to get lost in the world." Never mind the world, I mutter to myself, it's easy enough to get lost between Orlando and Lake Wales.

I sit down on a wrought iron bench to take it all in. I have to admit, Bok Tower Gardens is a relief from the hectic pace of the world. A bright red cardinal sings in the pine tree in front of me, and squirrels dash playfully across the path. After a few moments of reflection, I continue my walk.

Meandering along the Woodland Walk, down Mockingbird Walk past the Exedra (a semicircular place for conversation), I spot the Japanese Lantern. According to the monument nearby, the stone lantern was donated to the gardens by Usaburo Tsujita of Tokyo. A former member of Edward Bok's staff, Tsujita saved for seven years for the gift. It symbolizes a desire for world peace.

I am relaxed and refreshed as I move among the flowering shrubbery, reflecting ponds, and blossoming plants. I imagine it is like being in the Garden of Eden—peaceful, and divine.

In explaining his motives for building the gardens, Mr. Bok wrote that he wanted to create "a spot which would reach out in its beauty through the architecture of the tower, through the music of the carillon, to the people and fill their souls with the quiet, the repose, the influence of the beautiful..."

As I walk through the gardens toward the tower, I hear the bells ring out "Jesu, Joy of Man's Desiring" by Johann Sebastian Bach.

I feel dwarfed beneath the 205-foot tower that is reflected in its surrounding mote. It is made of pink marble, quarried in Georgia, and St. Augustine coquina. It is elegantly decorated. I raise my eyes to the frieze, thirty-two feet from the ground, that encircles the tower.

It depicts flamingos, pelicans, herons, and other Florida birds. Farther up the tower are beautiful grilles depicting sea creatures, land creatures, birds, and Adam and Eve.

Natalie Logan, the helpful information hostess, tells me that there are seven levels to the tower, although only the carillonneur is allowed into the tower itself.

"The tower was built to house the carillon," she explains, "which is an instrument composed of fifty-three bronze bells. The smallest bell weighs seventeen pounds. The largest weighs 22,300 pounds."

"How are the bells played?" I ask.

She pauses, looking at me. "With a keyboard," she answers. "The carillonneur, Milford Myhre, strikes the keyboard with his fists or his feet. The key pulls a wire attached to the clapper of a bell."

I sit on a bench shaded by a live oak tree and listen to the heavenly music filling the gardens. My mind, at last, is emptied of thoughts of deadlines, paychecks, car repairs, termites, overdrawn accounts, telephone bills, cockroaches, and other trivia of the outside world.

Edward Bok died on January 9, 1930. He is buried in front of the great brass door near the entrance of the tower. "Wherever your lives may be cast," his grandmother had once instructed her children, "make you the world a bit better or more beautiful because you have lived in it."

I wander through the gardens that Edward Bok created for all of us to enjoy. From the Live Oak Grove there is a commanding view of Lake Wales and the surrounding citrus groves. From the tower, the bells are playing Wolfgang Amadeus Mozart's "Papageno's Air" from *The Magic Flute*.

I stop at the Sunset Overlook. Before me the sky turns a spectacular mauve. Shafts of light ignite the low-lying clouds to the west as the bells from the tower play the ethereal "Lead, Kindly Light," by John B. Dykes. I imagine for a moment leaving my body behind and floating weightlessly above the gardens. The wind ruffles my hair and I spread my arms and take flight, circling the top of the tower like a dove. I soar over the countryside, high above the lakes and hills of Lake Wales.

"The Gardens, once entered," wrote landscape architect William Lyman Phillips, "affects the senses of the visitor gratefully, creates a poetic mood, induces feelings of reverence, stirs the mind to rapt admiration. Here voices are hushed as in a church . . ."

"Amen," adds the Tropical Son. "Amen."

A BIRD
IN THE BUSH

I went birding with writer Don Stap at Tosohatchee State Reserve. Tosohatchee is located approximately twenty miles east of Orlando, near Christmas, on State Road 50. The reserve consists of 28,000 acres of forest and marsh, bordered on the east by the St. Johns River. The state of Florida purchased the property in 1977 to preserve its unique plant and animal life. The public may hike, camp, fish, and enjoy many other outdoor activities on the reserve.

Don Stap agreed enthusiastically to go with me to Tosohatchee State Reserve for a hike and to talk about his book, *A Parrot Without a Name: The Search for the Last Unknown Birds on Earth.*

We both looked forward to seeing what kind of bird life existed at Tosohatchee. Before setting out for the reserve, I called Charlie Matthews, the park manager of Tosohatchee State Reserve, to find out what sorts of birds could be found in that area.

In addition to the more common species, he told me, "we have several nests of the American bald eagle. This past year we had seven active nests."

I was excited. The bald eagle is the national symbol of our country, and the adult's distinctive white head and tail make it unmistakable. I'd seen a handful in my lifetime, but the thought of seeing one so close to Orlando had a strange allure.

In the early afternoon, Don and I turned off of State Road 50 in Christmas and followed Taylor Creek Road to the headquarters of Tosohatchee State Reserve. At the entrance to the reserve, we picked up a bird list compiled by Robert E. Goble. It listed birds observed at Tosohatchee by Goble from 1985 to 1987. The list included everything from herons, ibises, and turkeys to owls, swallows, and yellow-billed cuckoos.

Don's book, *A Parrot Without a Name*, was published by Knopf in 1990. It chronicles two ornithological expeditions to the rain forests of South America: one with John O'Neill down the Shesha River and the other with Ted Parker in remote northern Peru. These two ornithologists from Louisiana State University have identified numerous new species of birds in the Amazon basin of Peru.

Don and I parked our car in a grove of longleaf pines and found the beginning of the hiking trail near Tosohatchee Creek. It was chilly out when we started hiking, but that didn't seem to discourage the mosquitoes. We followed the trail through thick stands of cabbage palms and pine trees. According to the Florida Department of Natural Resources, some of the pines in this area are over 250 years old. The ground was damp in places and ferns grew in profusion. The forest was alive with birds, and we paused to watch an armadillo nosing around in the brush.

"When did you first get interested in birds?" I asked Don as we walked along the trail.

"My mother gave me a bird book when I was about eight or nine," he said. "I found it fascinating that I could look in the book and see exactly what bird it was, its name, a map showing where it went in the winter."

Don cocked his head, listening to the sound of a bird

calling from the underbrush, then continued. "Years later, when I got to graduate school, I discovered this migratory bird refuge about forty-five minutes north of Salt Lake City called Bear River. There was a tremendous variety of birds there. I started going there a lot, paying more attention to birds, and getting more books."

We fell silent for a moment as Don pointed to a small bird flitting about in the bush. We both raised our binoculars for a closer look. The bird had a bright yellow rump with streaks of white and brown on the wings and tail. Don made a swishing sound with his lips, and the bird answered him with a sharp "Check!"

"That's a yellow-rumped warbler," he said. "Also known as a myrtle warbler."

I dutifully recorded its name in my notebook.

Don Stap received his doctorate from the University of Utah, and currently teaches English at the University of Central Florida. But he does not fit the stuffy academic mold. Don grew up in the farm country of southwestern Michigan. He is six-foot-two, and a soft-spoken, sandy-haired lover of the outdoors. Don is modest about his many achievements, which include a fellowship in poetry from the National Endowment for the Arts in 1986. As a free-lance journalist, he has written numerous articles on natural history for such magazines as *Sierra*, *International Wildlife*, and *Travel & Leisure*.

"When did you first meet the two ornithologists you wrote about in *A Parrot Without a Name?*" I asked.

Don said that when he was free-lancing in 1985, he called Ted Parker in Baton Rouge, Louisiana, to get some information about a place called the Explorer's Inn in Peru. "In the middle of the conversation he told me that he was doing some studies in Peru for the ornithology program at Louisiana State University. LSU had been involved in South American bird studies for twenty-five years."

We paused to look at a pair of holes drilled into a pine

tree by pileated woodpeckers. "LSU had discovered
about a dozen new species of birds in the last twenty
years. I was flabbergasted. I wrote John O'Neill, who
directs the program at LSU, and said I'd like to write an
article on this."

Don Stap went to Baton Rouge to talk to the ornithologists in December 1984. "As soon as I spent some
time with them, I knew that I had a dream project. They
invited me to go along at that point on an expedition."

On one of these expeditions, a new parrot was discovered. After the discovery, Don Stap wrote: "I cannot
believe my luck....Less than eighteen hours before I
must leave camp, O'Neill has a new species in his hand.
I could not be more surprised and delighted if a jaguar
came out of the forest and sat at my feet." The bird
belongs to the genus *Nannopsittaca*. The parrot without
a name is now known as the Amazonian parrotlet. Its
scientific name is *Nannopsittaca dachilleae*.

As we followed the trail deeper into Tosohatchee
State Reserve, Don said: "I always felt that I was privileged to have a chance to write about Parker and O'Neill.
They could have picked a far better-known writer than
me to write this story."

But book reviews indicate that the ornithologists
knew exactly what they were doing when they picked
Stap to write the book. The *New York Times* called the
book "Absorbing, eloquent, fascinating...packed with
intellectual and emotional joy." *Booklist* wrote that it
"will enthrall nature lovers and conservationists." And
Audubon Magazine said that the book was, "The ulti-
mate page-turner for anyone interested in the romance of
birds and discovery." The University of Texas Press has
now issued the book in paperback.

We followed the trail deeper into the forest. There is
a 900-acre virgin cypress swamp in the interior of
Tosohatchee that is said to be one of the most extensive

tracts of uncut cypress in the South. There is also a virgin tract of slash pine. I was secretly hoping that we would stumble across some unknown species of Florida avifauna. I was already mentally composing titles for my book: *A Vulture Without a Name: The Search for the Last Unknown Buzzards in Florida.*

At one point we crossed a road cut through the forest to accommodate power transmission wires. At the top of one of the power poles was an enormous nest of wood and twigs. Perched nearby was a large bird. Its white head made me think at first that it was one of the bald eagles I was hoping to see.

"Look," I yelled excitedly. "A bald eagle."

Don smiled gently and shook his head. "Osprey," he said as he raised his binoculars to his eyes.

The osprey is a large bird of prey that fishes in rivers, lakes, and along the coast. It is often seen hovering over water, its wings flapping violently. Then suddenly it dives feet-first to snag a fish.

Twilight was coming to Tosohatchee State Reserve. As I watched Don Stap look across the clearing at the osprey, I remembered a poem from his book, *Letter at the End of Winter.* Don wrote:

> *All day I followed the honking of geese*
> *until finally I saw them breaking above the trees*
> *in gray winter twilight, and then turning away*
> *the stitches coming loose*
> *until they were gone and I just stood there*
> *hands in my pockets.*
> *Green scarf around my neck.*
> *Looking.*

Although we made no new discoveries, I enjoyed my day at Tosohatchee State Reserve with the author of *A*

Parrot Without a Name. I can still picture Don Stap standing in the glow of the setting sun against the backdrop of longleaf pines and cabbage palms, his binoculars raised to his eyes...looking!

FLORIDA HISTORY

Wren and I were at a New Year's party when an "expert" on the Sunshine State, who had moved here a year earlier, made a sweeping arc with his hand to include all of Florida, and stated contemptuously, "The problem with Florida is that it has no culture, no history."

I'd heard that line before. The statement is often made by a confident newcomer who believes that history in Florida begins with the opening of Disney World in 1971.

Nothing is more annoying than this misrepresentation of the state. Florida can be accused of many things, but to say that it has no history is absurd. I cannot think of a state in the Union that has played a more rich and colorful role in U.S. history than Florida. Yet, I appreciate it when a remark like this comes up in a situation that gives me an opportunity to do what I enjoy most— lecture.

Florida history was a required course when I was in school. We studied the Native Americans, Spanish, French, English and their respective roles in settling the state. I relished the tales of pirates, smugglers, Confederates, and astronauts, all of whom have played a part in

Florida's history. The subject continues to fascinate me.

"No history?" I asked incredulously.

The people around us nodded in tacit agreement or mumbled something about "up North."

That was my cue. "No history?" I held the "i" in history to accentuate my Southern drawl. Heads turned my way as I plunged forward, playing the yokel. "What y'all mean?"

A snicker went around the circle of people and the speaker looked at me. "You see . . ." he began paternally, "the state I come from was founded by the Pilgrims, who established a colony at Plymouth in 1620. We have historic buildings and monuments. What do you have but tacky tourist shops, fast food restaurants, Mickey Mouse? There's no culture here, no sense of the past."

"What year you say these pilgrims came?"

"In 1620!"

I scratched my chin histrionically and tugged at my mustache. "Well, when your state was still 'undiscovered,' John Cabot spotted Florida. That was in 1498. He was the first European to see the state of Florida."

My opponent was unimpressed. "See the state?" he asked, meaningfully emphasizing "see."

"Yeah. Then about fifteen years after that, in 1513, Ponce de Leon landed somewhere between St. Augustine and Daytona Beach." I paused for effect. "You have heard of Ponce de Leon?"

Silence.

"Of course when Ponce de Leon arrived there were indigenous people living in nearly every region of Florida. The Timucuans lived in Central Florida. The Apalachee and the Tocobaga inhabited the north. In South Florida there were the Calusa and Tequesta. These were just a few of the tribes that had inhabited the peninsula thousands of years before the Europeans."

I took a sip of my beer and addressed the small group

gathered around us. "After all, to discount the Native Americans and their history in our state is an ethnocentric view whose time has passed. Don't you agree?"

I didn't give him time to answer before I continued. "Now back when Plymouth was no more than a pile of rocks, Tristan de Luna established a settlement near Pensacola in 1559." I looked at the man who had started the conversation. "That was sixty-one years before the colony was established at Plymouth. You want history?" I asked, warming to my subject. "Do you know what the first permanent city in the United States of America was?"

By now I was drawing either hostile stares or smiles of appreciation for having finally addressed the silly notion that Florida "has no history."

"St. Augustine," I answered my own question. "It is the oldest permanent city in the U.S. and was founded in 1565 by Pedro Menendez de Aviles—over half a century before Plymouth, and forty-two years before Jamestown, which was the first permanent English settlement."

My friend looked around feebly for support.

Since the history of the United States is written from an English point of view, we often forget that the Spanish were colonizing parts of the U.S. long before the English, and that the French settled at the mouth of the St. Johns River even before the Spanish.

Spain finally relinquished Florida to Britain in 1763 in exchange for Cuba—a country that continues to play a significant role in Florida's history, and always will.

Florida remained loyal to Britain during the American Revolution. When the thirteen colonies declared their independence in 1776, Florida did not join them. Seven years later the Spanish were back in Florida. But in 1821, Spain finally ceded its Florida land holdings to the United States.

"Florida became a state," I continued, "in 1845 and withdrew from the Union in 1861 to join the Confederacy." I took another sip of my beer. "The rest, as they say, is history."

"I haven't seen any monuments to all this so-called history," he snarled.

"Apparently you haven't looked very hard," I shot back. "There is a stretch of Florida's coast from Ormond Beach to St. Augustine that is one of the most scenic parts of coastal Florida left on the Atlantic. If you want to see some remnants of Florida's history, take in this stretch of the Atlantic coast. Just above Ormond are the ruins of the Bulow Plantation. Stop off at Washington Oaks Gardens north of Flagler Beach. Marineland gives you a glimpse of Florida's tourists attractions the way they used to be. Marineland is a tiny town on State Road A1A with only one industry—the Marineland aquarium located directly on the Atlantic Ocean, where you can see many varieties of sea animals. Even though this is a modern facility, it has an atmosphere reminiscent of an earlier time. Between Marineland and St. Augustine are some of Florida's most pristine beaches and historic sites. Hamlets like Summer Haven have not been built up the way most of Florida's east coast has. Fort Matanzas National Monument is a small fort built by the Spanish to defend the Matanzas River which leads to St. Augustine. More than 330 Frenchman were massacred here by the Spanish in 1565. The fort can be reached at no cost by a small boat run by the state park system."

I took a deep breath and plunged forward. "Finally, visit the St. Augustine area. The town of St. Augustine is a living museum of life during the Spanish colonial period. Extensive restoration has preserved the quaint houses and narrow streets of old St. Augustine. The Castillo de San Marcos was begun by the Spanish in 1672. It took over fifteen years to finish."

By the time I finished sharing this information, I had lost my audience. Only one defenseless senior citizen remained listening to me. She fumbled with the controls on her hearing aid. "What?"

I gesticulated wildly, reenacting de Soto's march inland from Tampa along the peninsula in search of the Fountain of Youth.

"Youth," I hollered.

"What?"

"The fountain of youth," I screamed into her ear.

The host of the party came over. He was a polite, well-dressed man. He looked knowingly at the beer can in my hand. My wife had long since disappeared and was probably denying that she knew me.

"It's late," the host suggested.

I looked around for the know-it-all who had gotten me started by asserting that Florida had no history. But he had apparently left.

With the finesse of a Southern gentleman, I agreed that, yes, it was late. But I was satisfied. I had vanquished the cad who had slandered the honor of the Sunshine State.

At least, I reasoned, the next time he voiced an opinion on Florida, he would make sure that there were no natives within earshot, or anyone else intelligent enough to know that Florida had inspired pirates, conquerors, adventurers and dreamers long before Walt Disney.

No history...indeed!

MAD DOGS AND ENGLISHMEN

I get up early Saturday morning, put on a warm sweater, wool cap, gloves, hiking boots, and grab a pair of binoculars. I am heading to the beach.

Most people don't think of going to the ocean in Central Florida during the cooler months. But that is my favorite season for the beach. That's right, and the colder the better.

I am not a lie-out-in-the-sun-and-develop-melanoma type of person. I have worked outdoors for at least half of my life beneath the Florida sun. My idea of relaxation is to get out of the sun and away from the crowds, either beside a shady spring or in some quiet woods. As Noel Coward observed, only "mad dogs and Englishmen go out in the midday sun."

Don't get me wrong. I love the sea and the beach, especially on a cold winter day when even Canadians have retreated indoors. I like to walk along the shore, watching the pelicans twirl downward after fish, and listen to the screech of the gulls.

The morning is cold. I pack a couple sandwiches and a thermos of water. I slip back into the bedroom and kiss my wife, Wren, goodbye. She turns over and mumbles some disparaging remark about my mental health, then falls back into dreamland.

I drive east on State Road 50 into the rising sun. At
Titusville I turn left on U.S. 1 and follow the Indian
River for about three and a half miles to State Road 406.
Here a bridge arches over the Intracoastal Waterway.
On the other side is Merritt Island National Wildlife
Refuge, which is the gateway to Canaveral National
Seashore and to one of the most beautiful stretches of
beach in the state of Florida.

Canaveral National Seashore was created in 1975 to
permanently protect its miles of pristine beach. Here I
can enjoy the ocean and shore without cars, condomini-
ums, and hotdog stands. Ironically, this unspoiled area
is adjacent to Kennedy Space Center. The nesting areas
of numerous endangered and threatened species lie within
the shadow of NASA's launching pads.

I stop at the Merritt Island National Wildlife Refuge
Visitor Information Center for some background information. The wildlife area was established in 1963 as a
sanctuary for migratory waterfowl. It is located along
the Atlantic flyway, a major route for birds that breed as
far north as the tundra of Canada and Alaska and spend
their winters as far south as the Caribbean. Some birds
migrate up to 6,000 miles, and this journey can take as
little as a week if conditions are favorable.

Various hiking and driving trails allow visitors to
explore the mangrove islands, marsh, pinewoods, la-
goons of shallow brackish water, beds of aquatic grass,
and the hardwood hammocks of the wildlife refuge and
Mosquito Lagoon. It is possible to see alligators, bobcats, raccoons, armadillos, and manatees. There are also
numerous wading birds, such as great blue herons, and
roseate spoonbills, as well as ospreys and bald eagles.

Beyond the information center, I enter the Canaveral
National Seashore, turn left on the paved road that runs
parallel to the shore behind the dunes, and follow it until
it reaches a dead end. I park in the last parking area of
Playalinda Beach and step up on the wooden crosswalk

by which visitors enter the beach. These crosswalks prevent destruction of the sea oats, seagrape, beach sunflower and any of the other 700 species of plants that grow in Canaveral National Seashore.

From the top of the dune, I look out at the sparkling Atlantic. The water is dark blue near the shore and frothing with whitecaps. Farther out it becomes aqua and blue-green. The air is fresh and tinged with the smell of saltwater. Looking up and down the beach, I see it just as it was when the Timucuans, who built their burial mounds and shell middens nearby, first saw it.

I walk down to the water's edge. I am glad I have my warm sweater on, for a cold wind blows off of the choppy Atlantic. The beach is nearly deserted. Only a surf fisherman, hundreds of yards up the beach, stands beside his fishing pole, which he has driven into the sand. These fisherman catch pompano, whiting, shark, and many other varieties of fish. But in winter, they're after bluefish.

Playalinda is Central Florida's unsanctioned, but well-known, nude beach. The temperature today is a brisk forty-nine degrees, so I am unable to catch a glimpse of that rare and elusive subspecies—the naked sunbather. Disappointed, I continue my hike in search of other wildlife.

Someday, I plan to hike the nearly twenty miles of deserted beach from Playalinda to the northern access point of Canaveral National Seashore, Apollo Beach, near New Smyrna. But today I am content to stroll along and watch a tiny sanderling, the smallest of the sandpipers, race after the receding waves on its rapid sticklike legs.

Using my binoculars, I watch a royal tern plunge into the sea. A school of dolphins surfaces briefly, then breaks free of a wave. Whales are occasionally spotted offshore, but I see only dolphins today.

I continue walking, occasionally stooping to pick up

shells. The Atlantic auger is an easy one to identify. It is a long, tapering shell. There are others as well: slipper shells, angel wing, calico scallop, lightning whelk, and coquina clam, the most common shell found on Florida's beaches. I am not a collector. I pick them up, admire them, and skip them back into the sea.

Toward noon, I sit down with my pack of sandwiches and watch a large, white ibis with black-tipped wings, red legs and a curved red beak pick its way along the shore. As I listen to the pounding of the surf, I am reminded of the power of nature at Canaveral National Seashore. There are strong currents on this beach, not to mention Portuguese man-of-war and jellyfish. As the tide begins to creep in, I also remember that a hike on the beach must be timed carefully so that one is not stranded by high tide. I take out my thermos and enjoy a drink. Of course, there are no drinking fountains or fresh water of any kind.

Much later, as the sun sets over Mosquito Lagoon, the sky turns salmon and a small crab scuttles toward the water. Walking back to my car, I think of Ft. Lauderdale beach to the far south. At spring break it is crawling with adolescent revelers. I think of Daytona Beach to the north during bike week, its shores jammed with bikers. Thanks to the National Park Service, Canaveral National Seashore's stretch of unspoiled beach, dunes, estuary, marsh, and creatures are preserved for those who enjoy the outdoors in its natural state.

Wren says I'm strange because I like to get bundled up and go to the beach in winter. I answer her cryptically, "Only mad dogs and Englishmen go out in the midday sun."

THE WITHLACOOCHEE WITH WILD BILL

*T*he airboat hurtles toward the solid wall of green vegetation on the opposite shore, then careens around a bend in the river. A flock of white herons takes flight and a pair of softshell turtles sunning themselves on a log plop into the water. The roar of the engine subsides as the captain cuts it, and we drift into a patch of water hyacinths.

"Look straight ahead," he says, pointing to a floating island of purple hyacinths.

I look but see nothing. Then a ripple in the water reveals the head of a four-foot alligator directly in front of us. The gator turns and stares at us with listless, hooded eyes, then lethargically sinks, only to surface a few feet farther away.

I am on the Withlacoochee River with Wild Bill MacKay.

Bill and Susan MacKay are the owners and operators of Wild Bill's Airboat Tours and Wilderness River Nature Safaris. Before buying a home on the Withlacoochee River in Citrus County, they were yacht charter captains in the Caribbean for ten years. When they decided they were ready for more stability than a yacht adrift in the Caribbean afforded, they moved to the small town of

Rutland in west Central Florida. The area is an outdoor paradise on the Tsala Apopka Chain of Lakes and the Withlacoochee River.

"Now what do we do?" they wondered. "There are no yachts around here."

There were no yachts but there were plenty of air-boats that the locals use to get into hard-to-reach marshes and swamps as well as navigable parts of the Withlacoochee. So, in 1989 Bill and Susan decided to begin an airboat tour. Since then they have had thousands of satisfied customers.

I had called earlier and made arrangements to meet Susan and Wild Bill MacKay. Even though it was raining, with no sign it was going to stop, Wild Bill told me to come on out. "I'll be glad to talk to you, and if the weather clears, we'll go out in the airboat," he said by phone. But as I drove west on State Road 44 toward the Gulf of Mexico, I was not sure what to expect from someone with a name like Wild Bill.

As it turns out, Wild Bill's moniker is more intimidating than the man. Bill MacKay is a teddy bear of a man, heavily built, with a round, happy face, sandy hair, and a ruddy outdoors complexion. He is at no loss for words when it comes to talking about all of the wildlife in his backyard (which is the Withlacoochee River itself). Both he and his soft-spoken wife, Susan, describe the animals in the surrounding forest as if they are friends.

Wild Bill gets wild only when he talks about the state-sanctioned alligator hunt, which he vehemently opposes. An outspoken defender of the alligator, Bill asks rhetorically: "If there's a problem between a person and a gator, guess who caused the problem?"

I do not feel compelled to answer.

Susan MacKay fetches me a yellow slicker (foul-weather gear she used in the Caribbean, she tells me, as if it will bring me luck) and I climb aboard the airboat.

Bill and Susan advertise their wilderness safari as "An Easy Adventure." It is. Despite the reputation of airboats as noisy, disruptive, and driven by crazed swamp rats, airboats are an exciting way to see remote parts of the Withlacoochee River.

A baby purple gallinule has boarded the boat before us, and Bill gently takes the little bird in hand and places it on shore.

Then he cranks the 500-cubic-inch Cadillac engine and the airboat roars to life. "I have a seventy-eight-inch prop on this boat," Bill tells me. "These large props spin slower and make less noise."

Actually, it is not as loud as I had expected. While the engine is idling, we can easily carry on a conversation. Nevertheless, Bill clamps on ear protectors and guns the engine, and we move out into the Withlacoochee River.

There are actually two Withlacoochee Rivers in Florida that are not to be confused. In North Florida, the Withlacoochee originates in Georgia and flows into the Suwannee River near the Georgia/Florida state line. We are on the "south" Withlacoochee River. The headwaters of the eighty-six-mile-long Withlacoochee are in the Green Swamp of northern Polk County. The river flows north and empties into the Gulf of Mexico near Yankeetown.

"Withlacoochee," Bill says over the roar of the engine, "means 'little great water.' As you can see, it is great water now," and he points to the flooded banks of the river, which is swollen from the recent rains.

We skip across patches of hydrilla, hyacinths, and even protruding logs. "All I need," Bill yells, "is an eighth of an inch of water."

Nevertheless, we stay mostly toward the middle of the river. Bill cuts the engine and, pointing to a floating mass of vegetation near the bank, explains why. "See there. That's a gallinule's nest."

I see a brown nest of twigs and brush floating on the water. Five or six of the baby gallinules (they look like little brown herons) waddle after their mother on their long sticklike legs across the vast beds of hydrilla and hyacinths.

Back out on the river, Bill's love of nature becomes even more evident as he points out the abundant wildlife. He looks among the dense forest of cypress trees on the watery banks of the river for the fourteen-foot mother alligator that he has named Snaggletooth . Up ahead, he points to a pair of huge osprey nests in the top of a cypress tree and a family of turtles sunning on a log.

"What other kinds of wildlife have you seen along the river?" I ask Bill as he turns the airboat into a shallow tributary of the main river.

"Turkey, wild boar, wildcats, deer, bear, ospreys, jaguarundi, coyotes."

"C'mon? Coyotes?"

"Yes. Awhile back I came across a deer that was stuck in the mud and there was a pack of coyotes around it, waiting for the kill. I scared the coyotes off, and the deer finally got out of the mud and ran away."

"Amazing." I knew that coyotes were still occasionally sighted in Central Florida, but that is rare, indeed.

"They even say there are monkeys back in the woods," Bill says.

I also knew that monkeys had escaped from an early shooting of *Tarzan* at Silver Springs and had reproduced and lived in the area near there. I wonder if these monkeys on the Withlacoochee might have come down from Silver Springs, but Bill isn't sure.

Bill and Susan's wilderness safaris are fifty minutes long. "We also give two-hour tours up to Blue Spring or Jumper Lake," he tells me.

Bill points to a red-shouldered hawk floating overhead. "I tailor each tour to the group. If I have older folks who want to take it slow, we do that. If they want to go faster, I move to the middle of the river and open her up."

Bill points to a brown bird with a large curving beak and feathers speckled with white. "That's a limpkin. The classiest bird on the river."

"Why do you say that?"

He turns the airboat back toward the center of the river. "Eats nothing but escargot."

Bill turns down another tributary of the river and points out an alligator nest on an island of vegetation. The cypresses are thick here and we must duck under their branches. Back on the main river, he turns the airboat toward home.

Skipping over the water like a stone tossed by a giant, I feel the exhilarating rush of air through my hair and the more exhilarating rush of having tasted once again from the overflowing cup of nature's beauty.

It is potent liquor!

FOUNTAIN OF YOUTH

I found the secret to eternal life in a small town north of Orlando. It's not really an original discovery. A lot of legwork had already been done before I got there.

Florida has always attracted people in search of a healthier, easier way of life, as if living here would somehow restore their youth. Perhaps that is why so many legends have surfaced concerning the Fountain of Youth. It may be the gentle breezes, the salt air, the warm climate that makes people think they are bound to live longer here. But I've always suspected it was the freshwater springs that held the secret of living forever.

History tells us that Don Juan Ponce de Leon of Spain "discovered" the peninsula of Florida in 1513. The king of Spain promised the explorer that he would make him the governor of the island of Bimini if he could find it. Bimini was believed to be a paradise with freshwater springs that would give people eternal youth. In addition, the king would give Ponce de Leon license to take any gold that he found there. Ponce de Leon never made it to Bimini. Instead, he landed somewhere between St. Augustine and Daytona Beach around Easter time. That was long before college kids had discovered the coast, so he didn't have to deal with the Spring Break crowds.

Historians claim that the search for the Fountain of Youth is a lot of bunk. They insist that Ponce de Leon was more interested in gold than any legendary fountain. But romantics maintain that he first heard the legend from a Carib Indian girl and that he searched for years for the magic waters of eternal youth. After all, Ponce de Leon was over fifty years old when he discovered Florida. You think about things like that at fifty.

These same romantics insist that the fountain is still out there somewhere. I believe it, and I'm not the only one. Even if Ponce de Leon wasn't interested in finding a fountain of eternal youth, thousands of people still come to Florida looking for a more youthful lifestyle. I'm thinking in particular of those who choose to retire in Florida. The demographics of America's search for eternal youth are interesting. According to the *Atlas of Florida,* "Before 1940 there was a smaller percentage of people 65 years and older in Florida than in the nation as a whole." However, after 1940 many older people began to retire to Florida. Today, "Florida has a higher percentage of people in the older age group than the United States as a whole." Maybe they know something the rest of us don't.

I have pursued an informal search for the Fountain of Youth for the past thirty-four years. That may seem like a strange pastime for an otherwise intelligent individual. But I don't plan to wait until I'm fifty to start grasping for ways to turn back the clock. Be honest—what if there were a magic spring where you could go, take a dip, and never have to worry about wrinkles again? Wouldn't it be worth a couple weekends to find it?

I'm not talking about the well-known attraction in St. Augustine, described by *Insight Guides of Florida:* "Past a stone arch with red neon lights that advertise the fountain, you will find a natural spring bubbling in a coquina shelter presumably of Spanish design. You will be offered a taste of spring water in a paper cup and can buy a whole bottle of the stuff at a gift shop. But don't be disappointed if you come away without feeling younger."

I already tried that. I walked around, took a sip from the fountain, checked out the statue of Ponce de Leon and toured the museum. I even bought a case of the stuff and drank a glass of it every morning at breakfast. Nothing!

No, I'm talking about the real Fountain of Youth. About nine miles northwest of DeLand on U.S. Highway 17-92 is the small town of DeLeon Springs and the DeLeon Springs State Recreation Area.

I entered the park through a set of ornate wrought iron gates with wrought iron lamps hanging from the stone pillars. The area around the spring was once a plantation named Spring Garden. It was settled in 1804 and planted with cotton, corn, and sugar cane. Colonel Orlando Reese (for whom Orlando is named) used the water bubbling up from the spring to run a mill for processing sugar cane. John James Audubon visited the Reese plantation in 1832.

Massive live oaks cast shadows across the grassy picnic areas and provide shade for those bathers seeking respite from the sun. The spring itself is a large, circular pool about sixty feet in diameter. Paddleboats, canoes, inner tubes, masks, fins, and snorkels can be rented for exploring the area. There is even a rustic eating place, the Old Spanish Sugar Mill Restaurant.

Initially I was disappointed. This was just not what I expected the Fountain of Youth to look like. I walked indolently about the grounds inspecting the remains of the sugar mill and ambled along the hiking trail. I watched canoes being launched into Spring Garden Creek that leads into the 18,000-acre Lake Woodruff National Wildlife Refuge adjoining the park. It was a beautiful place, but it didn't seem like the kind of place where man's most fervent desire—to live forever—was likely to be satisfied.

Then I took a dive into the water. It was a cold seventy-two degrees. Since it was about ninety-two outside, the water seemed particularly cold, and I was immediately refreshed. I swam for about an hour, diving down as far as I could into the translucent water to where the spring "boils" up from a cave underground. I floated languidly back and forth across the pool. I felt invigorated, energetic—well, yes, youthful!

Then a strange thing happened. I went to the changing rooms to get out of my wet swimsuit. Looking into the mirror, I seemed, somehow, trimmer. I turned for a side view and yes, my body seemed to have toned up a bit. I flexed my biceps and looked at myself over my shoulder. Then I noticed that the tiny wrinkles around my eyes had disappeared and the folds on my forehead were no longer there. I ran my hand through my hair. I was actually growing younger before the mirror.

How do I explain this? It might simply be the peaceful environment at DeLeon Springs and the brisk spring water that calmed my nerves and relaxed my muscles. However, early promoters of the spring claimed that the waters were "impregnated with a deliciously healthy combination of soda and sulphur."

Maybe I just imagined this transformation. But I go back as often as possible and I'm feeling younger all the time. Hey, it's worth a try. Admission to the park is a lot cheaper than plastic surgery.

Ponce de Leon never actually made it to the spring named after him. Too bad. He returned to Florida in 1521 with two ships carrying two hundred men. They landed near Port Charlotte, where they were attacked by

Indians. Ponce de Leon was wounded and died soon after in Havana. Had he found the spring, he might be around today to tell us what Florida was like in the 16th century. I'd like to hear some of those stories.

MOSS
PICKER

*T*here are times when I believe that the old
Florida is gone forever. That quiet evenings on the front
porch, listening to the music of the cicadas as the aroma
of orange blossoms wafts across the lake, are but a
distant and irretrievable memory. With the orange groves
mostly frozen out in my part of Florida, I am all too often
reminded by their dead trunks of the way things used to
be. I never thought much about orange groves when I
was growing up surrounded by them. Now I look back
with the kind of nostalgia that Marjorie Kinnan Rawlings
expresses so well in her book, *Cross Creek*. She writes:
"Enchantment lies in different things for each of us. For
me, it is in this: to step out of the bright sunlight into the
shade of orange trees; to walk under the arched canopy
of their jadelike leaves; to see the long aisles of lichened
trunks stretch ahead in a geometric rhythm; to feel the
mystery of a seclusion that yet has shafts of light strik-
ing through it. This is the essence of an ancient and
secret magic. . . . And after long years of spiritual
homelessness, of nostalgia, here is that mystic loveli-
ness of childhood again. Here is home."

I know that feeling well. But there are times when,
even as I sit out in the evenings on the land where I was
born, listening to the whippoorwills call to one another

across the lake, I feel that same homelessness, since my home of Florida is rapidly evolving into something else.

But something happened not long ago that reminded me that the "native" culture of old Florida still survives. I was sitting in the living room reading the Sunday paper when I heard someone drive onto the property. I looked up and saw a pickup coming down the long sand road that winds its way through what used to be our grove. Out where I live company is a major event. I put down the paper and went outside to see who it was.

The pickup was a rusted early-model Ford. There was a gun rack with a shotgun on it in the back window, and the bed of the truck was overflowing with moss.

Spanish moss is unique to the southeastern United States, and it has almost come to symbolize the Deep South. Spanish moss hangs from live oaks and other tree branches and even from telephone wires. Its range is primarily coastal, as far north as Virginia and as far west as Texas. Believe it or not, Spanish moss is in the pineapple family. Some people mistakenly believe that it is a parasite. But it is an epiphyte or air plant. It takes water and nutrients from the air and converts them to energy through photosynthesis.

A portly black man in his late thirties heaved himself from behind the wheel of the truck.

"How you doing?" I called.

He took off his straw Stetson and wiped his brow with his hand. "Hot," he answered.

In the country it is considered bad manners to directly address the issue at hand—a custom I find myself readjusting to after a week of work in the city.

First we talked about how hot it was. Then we talked about fishing, briefly, since my knowledge of the topic is limited. A boy got out of the passenger side of the truck. He was a handsome kid, barefoot and shirtless, about ten years old, and the man introduced him as his son. That provided another topic as the man expounded on the laziness of the younger generation.

Finally he said, "That's some tall bamboo you got there," and pointed to the fence line on the north side of the property that was overgrown with bamboo. On the old homesteads of Florida, bamboo was commonly planted along fence lines. This patch had been planted in the 1930's.

My own curiosity had gotten the best of me. "What are you doing with all that moss?" I asked.

"I'm a moss picker," he answered, as if it were obvious.

In earlier days, Spanish moss was used to stuff mattresses and pillows. I had read once about the moss-pickers of Louisiana. Many of them are Cajuns who go into the bayous in shallow canoes (or pirogues) and reach into the cypresses with long, hooked poles and pull moss from the trees. When their boats are filled, they bring the moss back to town to sell. But I was not aware that people still pursued this traditional trade in Florida.

"Where do you get the moss?" I asked.

He looked around us at the oaks drenched with moss, some strands hanging down and nearly touching the ground. "All over," he said. "Around here, down in Clermont."

"How do you pick it?"

His son giggled and his father gave him a sharp look, then smiled himself. They were probably thinking that anyone who didn't know how to pick moss must be pretty stupid.

"You see," the man began, "I get me a long pole and I reach up into the tree and pull it out. Fill up my truck and go home."

"What do you do with it?"

"Sell it."

"Where?"

"In Orlando."

Again I was struck by the incongruities of life in Florida. "What do the people you sell it to do with it?"

"Make paper out of it," he said.

As they say, you learn something new every day.

"So you want to get some of this moss?" I asked impatiently, indicating the oak trees in the yard and hoping to get to the point.

"No."

Somehow I was offended. Wasn't my moss good enough? Did I have some kind of low-grade moss or something? "There's plenty of it," I said hopefully.

"No, I got lots of moss."

I was stumped, but decided to let him get to the point in his own time.

"Yeah, I reach up into the trees with a big, long pole and pull it out of the trees," he said. "Fact, I need a new pole." He looked over at the fence line. "How long you reckon one of them bamboo poles are?"

"Pretty tall."

"I'd like to cut a piece of that if you don't mind."

"Sure, help yourself."

As if on cue, the boy grabbed a pruning saw from the seat of the truck and disappeared into the cane patch. In a flash he pulled out a bamboo pole about 25 feet long and expertly trimmed the clumps of leaves from it.

"Yeah, that's big bamboo," the man said. "But you ain't never seen bamboo like they got over there in Vietnam. It's big as your arm."

We chatted a while longer. He had been born and raised a few miles away, and we talked about the changes that had come to Florida.

About every two months the moss picker comes back to cut a new cane pole. I enjoy talking to him about the old times: good and bad. Where else but in Florida can two people in their thirties talk about the "old days"?

It's nice to know that some people still remember.

LIKE GOOD WINE

I am faced with a typical Floridian dilemma. My aunt Coletta is in town and I want to take her somewhere for an afternoon. She's been to all the attractions, and at seventy-five she's not exactly up to bushwhacking her way through the swamp on one of my outdoor adventures. Alligator farms are out of the question. The last time I took her to one, things got a little out of hand. But that, as they say, is a tune from another opera.

I labor for hours over the problem of where to take my aunt. Coletta is my mother's sister. The daughter of Irish immigrants, she's as mischievous as a leprechaun. But lately she's more drawn to a cup of tea by the fireplace than an afternoon safari into the wild interior of Florida with her tropical nephew.

Then it hits me. I think of a place that is out in the country, easily accessible, and will literally "give her a taste" of a newly emerging industry in Central Florida— the Lakeridge Winery.

California has its Napa Valley, and New York state has its wine regions. In Lake County, the fledgling Lakeridge Winery has a vision of turning thousands of acres of rolling hills covered with frozen orange groves into Florida's own wine country. It's an ambitious dream.

Today, at Lakeridge there are thirty-four acres of young vineyards and a winery. The vineyard manager, Jeff Gloss, intends to plant another seventy-five acres within the next three years. Visitors can tour the vineyards and winery seven days a week and sample any of the nine different wines produced there.

When I mention going to the winery, my aunt says, "I'm not much of a wine drinker. Now your mother and I liked a drop of Jameson's in the evening."

"Aunt Coletta, I don't think they have Jameson's there. This is a vineyard where they grow grapes and make wine."

"I'm not much of a wine drinker," she says again as if to convince herself. But Coletta's a good sport, and she agrees to the trip. Besides, there is no charge for the tour or sampling.

She likes that.

We head for the winery in the early afternoon. If you think of Florida as monotonously flat, you may be surprised by the rolling hills that surround the winery. These hills were once covered with thousands of acres of citrus groves until the devastating freezes of the 1980's.

We drive up the long sloping driveway between rows of grape trellises toward the Spanish colonial-style building that houses the winery.

According to the folks at Lakeridge, wine making in America began in Florida. That's news to me, but their argument is convincing. "The French Huguenots who reached North America between 1562 and 1564," we are told, "made wine from the wild muscadine grapes they found growing in abundance near the present site of Jacksonville, Florida. This is the first recorded reference of wine made from grapes in the New World."

Coletta is a loyal New Yorker and she's a little skeptical of this information. "Well, New York state makes some very good wine," she says defensively. "I didn't even know they grew grapes in Florida."

I let it pass. I don't bother to tell her that by the early 1900's, there were more than 5,000 acres of grapes growing in Central Florida, many of them in the area of the present-day Lakeridge Winery. The well-drained, sloping land (which provides sunny exposure) and the numerous lakes are ideal for growing grapes. Unfortunately, these non-native grapes were wiped out by Pierce's disease early in this century.

In 1923, the University of Florida established a program to develop disease-resistant varieties of hybrid bunch grapes. Wild muscadine grapes were cross-pollinated with European varieties to produce the Florida hybrid bunch grape.

We enter the gift shop and tasting room. We are greeted by a friendly hostess who tells us that a tour will begin in a moment. We take a few minutes to look around the shop. There are racks of wine, books on wine, and an assortment of gifts, wine accessories, and baskets.

Soon our hostess signals for us to follow her.

First we view a slide presentation that traces the history of Lakeridge Winery and Vineyards. "Establishing a vineyard is a labor-intensive task," we are told. The land is prepared with posts and wire, which serve as the framework of the vineyard's trellises. An irrigation system is installed. Then young grape vines are hand-planted and trained to grow along the trellises. The vines are carefully nurtured to promote healthy growth. In three to five years, when the vineyard is mature, it will yield about seven tons of grapes per acre. Each ton will yield about 550 bottles of wine.

"Wow," I say to my aunt. "I had no idea that one acre could produce so much wine."

The growing season begins in March. Warm spring days and nights, as well as breezes from the lakes, help promote the growth of the vines and development of the grapes. The vineyard is fertilized, irrigated, and sprayed for insects during this crucial period. By early July the grapes are ready to be harvested.

"Interesting," my aunt concedes as the slide presentation ends and we begin a walking tour of the winery itself. We stroll along an elevated walkway above the wine-making facility.

At the winery, the grapes are weighed, inspected, tested, and carefully examined by the wine maker, Jeannie Burgess, and her staff. The stems are removed from the grapes and the fruit is crushed and sent through a dejuicer, then into a continuous press. The juice is stored in stainless steel tanks, where solid particles, called lees, settle to the bottom and are later strained out. The skins and seeds are used as an organic fertilizer in the vineyard.

Yeast is added to begin the natural fermentation process. This slow fermentation process preserves the fruit's flavor and aroma. The wines are ready to bottle within six to eight months after harvest. The wine is bottled, sealed with natural cork, and allowed to rest briefly before being shipped to market. Lakeridge wines are "young wines." They do not age the wines.

We follow our hostess through the rest of the wine maker's laboratory and re-emerge in the gift shop and tasting room. We are directed to an oblong counter where wine glasses have been set out.

Our hostess starts the tasting session with a wine-tasting lesson. She pours us each a sample of Lakeridge's semidry Suwannee 1988.

"The first thing you want to remember when you're tasting chilled wine is not to hold your glass by the bowl. Hold it by the stem. If you hold the glass by the bowl, it warms the wine."

We dutifully hold our glasses by their stems.

"I'm not much of a wine drinker," my aunt reminds me for the third time.

"Next, hold your glass up to the light and look through the wine. Make sure it is clear, not cloudy."

We hold our glasses to the light, already feeling like connoisseurs.

"Swirl the wine around in your glass. What you are doing is releasing the bouquet. Now smell that fragrance."

Coletta's on familiar ground here. "They do this with brandy," she tells me, swirling her glass and sniffing.

We take a sip of our wine.

"Hold it on your tongue for a second," the hostess tells us. "Now take a second sip."

The wine has a soft, subtle flavor.

"The next wine I want you to try is our Classic White."

Coletta needs no encouragement this time. She pushes her glass forward for the next sample.

"Classic White is made from the muscadine grape. It's a little bit sweeter."

We take a sip. "That's good," I say.

Coletta has drained her glass. "It's liable to make us tipsy," she adds.

Next, our hostess pours us a sample of a wine called Flamingo. It is a "delicately colored but richly flavored wine," she reads from the label.

Coletta and I are into the spirit of it now, and are playing the part of critics. "Not bad," I offer.

"I've had better," she says.

The next wine is called Southern White. It is a "smooth, rich southern wine with full aroma and mellow flavor."

"Too fruity," I say, an expert now. It doesn't seem to bother my aunt. She downs her glass.

We finish with a taste of Southern Red. According to the label, this "garnet hued, light-bodied red derives its unique fruity flavor from the Noble grape. Slightly sweet for dinner, dessert, or just relaxing."

We finish our wine and move away from the counter. Coletta seems a little unsteady, but it may just be my imagination. It has been a fun day. I buy a bottle of the Cuvee Blanc which was awarded a silver medal at the International Eastern Wine Competition in Watkins Glenn, New York, in 1988. I read from the label: "The delightful flavor of this light-bodied, semidry blend of Stover and Suwannee makes it a natural partner to fish, poultry, and light dishes."

Coletta is examining the shelves and reaches for a bottle of the Blanc Du Bois. "I'm not much of a wine drinker," she starts to explain as she grabs the bottle.

I smile and nod approvingly. I'm thinking as I watch my aunt: Some things do get better with age.

AN AFTERNOON
WITH THE SENATOR

St. Bernard wrote in the 12th century: "You will find something more in woods than in books. Trees and stones will teach you that which you can never learn from masters."

I was thinking of this bit of wisdom one day last week as I left my office at the university. On my way home, I stopped at Big Tree Park in Seminole County to see what the trees there might teach me. I wanted to have a look at a most unusual attraction—a 3,500-year-old living cypress tree. If any tree had something to teach, surely it would be this one.

I turned off of U.S. Highway 17-92 in Longwood onto General J.C. Hutchison Parkway—a grandiose name for this two-lane road that passes through an area of wetlands east of State Road 427. A mile or two on the left, I entered Big Tree Park and pulled my car under the shade of a sprawling oak tree. The parking area is a narrow strip of woods alongside picnic tables, barbecue grills, and two covered dining areas. At the south end of the parking area is the beginning of a wooden board-walk. A sign reads: "Big Tree – 150 yards."

The land on which the largest cypress tree in the United States grows was donated to Seminole County by

Senator M.O. Overstreet. The tree is named "The Senator" in his honor.

I made my way along the boardwalk that winds through native Florida habitat. The afternoon was bright and chilly—a perfect day for a walk. Cabbage palms grew in profusion among the oaks, and tiny blue flowers bloomed in the spongy soil. Parts of the woods had been planted with sago palms, bromeliads, and shrimp plants. There were dense stands of bamboo. Orange trees, that were either wild or remnants of a former grove, were scattered throughout the forest. Because the soil was damp, there were many elderberry bushes. Dozens of birds chattered as I watched a squirrel and a blue jay fight over the spoils of the berry bushes.

I stopped to read the commemorative plaque that tells the history of Spring Hammock Nature Park. In 1927, Senator M.O. Overstreet donated the Big Tree Park site to Seminole County. It is on this site that the 3,500-year-old cypress tree—one of the world's largest known living cypress trees—stands. In the 1960's, the Seminole County League of Women Voters encouraged the county to acquire parklands. They were particularly interested in preserving the unique flora and fauna of the Spring Hammock area. As a result of their efforts, Soldier's Creek Park was purchased in 1974. In 1976, the Seminole County School Board and Board of County Commissioners sponsored the establishment of an Environmental Studies Center at Soldier's Creek Park. Today, this study center offers "multidisciplinary environmental education to more than 16,000 students" each year.

"So," I said to myself as I looked around, "I'm not the first to come here to learn from trees."

In 1980, the approximately 1,500 acres of Spring Hammock Nature Park were designated by the Department of Natural Resources as a high priority site for acquisition by the state. The CARL (Conservation and Recreation Lands) program was created "to preserve significant environmental lands through cooperation between private property owners and the State of Florida." Spring Hammock Nature Park contains an abundance of native Florida vegetation and provides habitat to a variety of Florida wildlife, including numerous endangered and threatened species of plants and animals. Physiographically, it is classified as a hydric hammock. Spring Hammock Nature Park also contains Indian and early settler archaeological sites. All of this offers unique educational and recreational opportunities to residents of Central Florida.

I continued walking along the boardwalk. Magnolia trees, with their shiny leaves, shaded the walk. The wet ground was covered with a carpet of ferns. Suddenly, through the trees I saw an enormous wall of wood looming up from the jungle. I raised my eyes along its length as I walked toward it. Although the signs had prepared me for a big tree, this giant cypress was beyond the scale of anything I had imagined. Standing at the base of the enormous tree, I leaned all the way back to see its top branches, and nearly fell over backward in the process.

The Senator is a 126-foot-tall Bald Cypress— *Taxodium distichum.* Its circumference is forty-seven feet. Its diameter is over seventeen feet. Its age, according to estimates of the American Forestry Association, is 3,000 to 3,500 years. There are approximately 50,000 board feet of lumber in the tree—a statistic that only a builder could possibly appreciate.

None of these vital statistics given on the plaque at the base of the tree manages to convey the grandeur of this ancient cypress. All the trees around it were dwarfed by comparison. One is easily reminded that the Senator is a living remnant of a prehistoric forest. A few cone-like cypress knees grew around the base, and vines struggled up its side. The sides of the Senator were gnarled and knotty, and a white scale grew on its rough, pockmarked bark. A cable ran down the side of the tree for conducting lightning safely into the ground. It is a wonder that the Senator had survived lightning storms for all these years. A fence donated by the Florida Federation of Garden Clubs in 1951 encircled the tree to protect it from vandalism. The tree is unbelievably awe-inspiring, even humbling.

I mused for a moment on what this tree had lived through. I revere things that are old—antiques, cars, people—because they are survivors. They've lived through times that most of us can only imagine. There are times when we need to reflect on the past, to acquaint ourselves with something ancient, and to learn from it. Trees and stones can teach you more than you can learn from masters, I thought to myself. What is it that we can learn from the Senator?

I looked up high into the frail branches of the tree as if seeking an answer. Cypress trees bloom in early spring with purple flowers. The Senator has small cones and green needlelike or fernlike leaves that seem pathetically stunted in comparison to its massive trunk.

"It's not a pretty tree," a voice said, startling me.

Beside me stood a well-dressed man in a business suit looking up at the Senator. "It's just unusual."

I turned my attention to him. He looked up at the Senator with a kind of reverence and then said, almost embarrassed, "I come out here to unwind when I've had a hard day at work."

I nodded toward the Senator. "It's magnificent, isn't it?"

The man looked at the tree as if it were a celebrity. "Yes, it is quite magnificent."

There is a second cypress tree a short distance from the Senator, but it has no name and is not similarly honored. I strolled over to inspect this equally magnificent cypress.

What can we learn from trees? I wondered again.

A plaque at the base of the Senator reads: "The National Arborist Association recognizes this tree and commends those who had the vision and foresight to preserve it."

This was what I learned from an afternoon with the Senator. It is thanks to the vision of a previous generation that we have this ancient and venerable living link to our prehistoric past right in the center of Metro-Orlando.

As I left Big Tree Park, I heard an owl call to me from the woods, "Whoo, whoo."

Even the birds had lessons to teach. "Who, who?" asked the owl. "Who will have the foresight and vision to preserve the remaining pieces of natural Florida for the enjoyment of generations three thousand years into the future?"

"We will," I said to the owl. "I hope we will."

A DISTANT NOVEMBER

There is one distant November day that nearly everyone in America over the age of thirty-five can remember. I remember it distinctly, because for a brief moment I saw myself as a stranger in the community that I had always called home.

Florida is a land of numerous ethnic, national, and religious communities. This diversity makes Florida unique among the Southern states. However, things have not always been like this. In 1963, the population of the state was less than half of what it is today. The citrus industry was still king in Central Florida, and Lake County, where I was born, was very much a rural, agricultural county.

At that time, the ethnic picture was two-sided. About twenty percent of the population was black and the rest was predominantly white. The vast majority of the people, black and white, belonged to protestant churches—overwhelmingly Baptist. Make no mistake about it, nearly everyone belonged to some church, for church was the social hub of the community.

My family was among the minority of Roman Catholics in our small town. Even the name of the religion sounded suspiciously foreign to some. The rumors that circulated around town concerning what Catholics actually "did" in their church were sources of amusement in our home. However, I was no less curious about what went on in the Baptist Church. But this was in the days before Vatican II had significantly changed the church. We still heard mass in Latin, and eating meat on Fridays was forbidden.

I remember one Sunday on the way home from mass passing the open doors of a Pentecostal church. A chorus of soulful voices seemed to set the little church shaking with joyful noise. The parishioners shook tambourines and cried out in spontaneous shouts of praise. Remembering the cheerless ritual of our mass, I looked longingly into the interior of this black church where the people praised their God so boisterously. But in those days, the interior of a protestant church was as distant to this little Catholic boy as the gates of heaven—or that other place.

Even though Catholics were a minority in this Southern town, I never felt mistreated. But we *were* misunderstood. I had been told by well-intentioned classmates that I had "dirt" on my face when I came to school late on Ash Wednesday with the symbolic ash that the priest had smudged, in the sign of the cross that morning at mass, on my forehead.

When I occasionally slept over at a protestant friend's house on Friday nights, his mother would dutifully serve me fish as the family dined on hamburgers. My friend could not quite believe that I voluntarily passed up burgers and fries in the name of religion. My own hazy understanding of theology, when communicated to him, was met with incredulity.

"Catholics don't eat meat on Fridays and they have lots of kids," seemed to be the sum of his parents' knowledge of the faith. And I was living proof of the stereotype—last of seven children, and a faithful vegetarian on Fridays.

But one November day made me proud of my own church. November 22, 1963, was a Friday. I was a seven-year-old boy, sitting in Mrs. Sullivan's first-grade class. I remember it was Friday because on Fridays I walked with the two other Catholic kids in our class to St. Mary of the Lakes Church for catechism, or religious instruction.

There was a warm comradeship among the three of us who walked to catechism. Carolyn's family had been in the parish for years, and Rosemary was a recently arrived immigrant from Germany. Rosemary had long, straight, blond hair that reached her waist, and an oddly charming way of speaking. Though I had a crush on her, she towered over me by several inches and treated me like a pesky little brother.

"Did you hear about President Kennedy?" one of them asked.

Although the details were not clear, we knew from rumors that had circulated at school that something terrible—we weren't sure quite what—had happened to the president.

In my Irish-Catholic home, President Kennedy's portrait hung over the mantle between pictures of Pope John XXIII and St. Patrick, staff in hand, treading on one of the snakes he had allegedly driven from Ireland. By association, John Kennedy was invested with a kind of divinity. In the mind of a seven-year-old, if he was not a saint, he was at least in the same ballpark as the saints, angels, archangels, and the rest of the dizzying array of players on the team of Roman Catholicism.

When the three of us arrived at the parish hall of St. Mary's that Friday, a dreadful gloom hung over the place. Catechism had been cancelled. Instead, two of the sisters, clothed in long black habits, led us into the sanctuary, where we knelt with all the assembled catechism classes.

One of the nuns stepped forward with her rosary

beads in her hand. "Boys and girls," she said. "Our president, John Kennedy, has been shot."

We knew what she meant when she said "our" president, and my heart ached with sorrow and pride. A few children began to sniffle, and I turned my face from Rosemary's so she wouldn't see the tears coming down my cheeks.

The sister kneaded her rosary and led us in a recitation of the five sorrowful mysteries. I blessed myself and clutched my sweaty palms together, thinking that nobody would dare tell the president of the United States that his face was dirty on Ash Wednesday. And on that distant day in November, I prayed, with the fervent devotion of a seven-year-old, for the soul of John Fitzgerald Kennedy.

BEAR
CROSSING

One night as Wren and I were driving along State Road 46, just west of the Wekiva River, we saw something lumber out of the woods and bolt across the road. I hit the brakes, and we came to an abrupt halt. Into the patch of light given off by our headlamps stepped a Florida black bear. It seemed like a young bear, judging by its size, and it had a dark, healthy coat. The bear did not linger, but dashed into the swampy woods on the other side of the road.

For a moment, Wren and I sat stunned. We had unexpectedly sighted one of the most unusual creatures in Florida, and the largest native mammal in the state. The area where we spotted the bear was well sign-posted as a bear crossing. In 1988 alone, nine bears were killed by automobiles on State Road 46.

We had seen the bear close to the entrance of Rock Springs Run State Reserve. I decided to go back and explore this little-known state reserve about thirty miles north of Orlando. I wanted to find out what kind of habitat the Florida black bear prefers and to see what signs of bears I might find in the Wekiva River Basin.

The entrance to the reserve is located eight miles west of Interstate 4. I turned off State Road 46 onto

County Road 433, which dead-ends at the entrance to the reserve.

Rock Springs Run State Reserve's 12,000 acres borders more than twelve miles of the Wekiva River and Rock Springs Run. The land was acquired by the state of Florida in 1983 to preserve native wildlife habitat, protect the water in the area, and offer outdoor recreational opportunities for the citizens of the state. The reserve is open to the public from 8 a.m. to sunset. Hiking, canoeing, nature study, and horseback riding are encouraged. There is even a primitive camping area on Rock Springs Run.

I picked up a map of the reserve at the parking area and began my hike in the late morning. I shouldered my pack and followed the sand road into the heart of the reserve. A sign near the entrance of the reserve reports that there are twenty-three black bears living in the Wekiva River Basin. This may not seem like many. In fact, it is far fewer than are needed to sustain a self-sufficient population.

Bears need an incredible amount of space in which to forage and roam if they are to survive. One female bear requires twelve square miles; a male bear needs over forty square miles. The bears in the Wekiva River Basin can only survive if they are able to cross State Road 46 and travel north into the Ocala National Forest. The Department of Natural Resources has been actively acquiring land between the Wekiva River Basin and the Ocala National Forest to preserve a travel corridor for wildlife. If these corridors are not preserved, the black bear faces local extinction on some lands south of the Ocala National Forest. Already the black bear is a threatened species throughout most of Florida.

I walked along the sand road that leads into the reserve. The area at the beginning of this trail is composed mostly of sand pine scrub and green seas of palmettos. I soon came to a point where several roads come together, but I continued walking straight on Spear Road in hopes of eventually reaching the primitive campsite on Rock Springs Run—about a two hour hike.

The left side of Spear Road had been extensively burned by state biologists and reserve rangers as part of their management program. This was a low area with patches of wetland and pools of water standing amid pines, palmettos, and tufts of wire grass. The smell of smoke hung in the air. I scanned the ground for bear tracks but could only see where a few deer had crossed the sand road.

Black bears are extremely shy animals, so I did not expect to see one. However, there are several things to look for as evidence of the presence of bears: torn-apart logs, broken trees, marked trees, tracks, and scats (droppings).

Bear tracks look strikingly similar to prints left by humans. Like humans, bears have five toes, although only four are usually visible in the print. Often the bear's hind feet step into or over the prints of their front feet. But the track of the Florida black bear is unmistakable due to its size.

The day was hot and the sky brilliant. I entered an area of pine flatwoods. Beside the road stagnant pools of copper-colored water, their bottoms lined with pine needles, glinted in the sun.

Soon the stands of pine began to thicken. I could tell I was getting near the river because tall palm trees raised their shaggy heads above the forest. I stopped again to examine tracks where a deer had crossed the road. But I found no bear tracks.

Occasionally I would see a small tree bent over in the woods. Then I saw other trees that had been broken in half. These bent and broken trees are also signs that bears have been in the area. Bears bend over small oak trees to get to the acorns at the top. As for the pine trees, some experts believe that young bears climb these small pine trees and playfully sway back and forth on them.

I examined one of the pine trees for slash marks where a bear might have scratched and bitten the tree as he rubbed against it. Bears rub against trees not only to scratch themselves but also to shed or to leave a scent for other bears. I looked closely at the barks of several trees to see if I could spot pieces of hair, but I found none.

After about an hour and a half of walking, the right-hand side of the road became a dense, marshy hammock of palmettos, magnolias, ferns, cypress trees, needle palms, and bamboo. I saw the listless eyes of an alligator stare up from one of the dark pools of water beside the road. As I moved closer, it slithered farther into the swamp.

Again I scanned the road for bear tracks. Then I spotted a pine tree that had been torn apart by a bear. Bears eat acorns, blueberries, huckleberries, gallberries, blackgum berries, and palmetto fruit. But they will also rip apart rotten trees to eat the insects inside.

Although bears will run whenever they see people, I shivered slightly at the sight of the torn-apart tree. I was probably five miles from my car by now and deep into the Rock Springs Run State Reserve. I looked near the torn-up pine tree for bear scats. But there was no other evidence of the bear's presence.

I recalled some more of the information I had gleaned from the sign at the beginning of the trail. A female usually has her first cubs when she is between three and four years old. After that she can have a litter of two to four cubs every two years. Her cubs will stay with her for about a year and a half. It is interesting that adult females remain in the area where they were born. Males, on the other hand, leave the area to establish their own territory.

Female bears in Florida weigh between 150 and 200 pounds, while males average 250 to 350 pounds. Looking around uneasily, I wondered if it were a male or female bear that had torn this tree apart. If it were a female, there might be cubs nearby. Suddenly I heard a tremendous crash and something broke out of the brush in front of me. I jumped back, my heart pounding, and fell over backward. My heart itself was beating in my rib-cage like a wild beast trying to escape. I looked up, terrified, as an armadillo scampered from the thicket and walked placidly across the trail.

My breathing was heavy as I tried to calm my nerves. Little animals sure can make a big noise, I said to myself, the adrenaline still roaring through me. I got up on shaky legs and continued my hike.

Eventually I came to the primitive campsite where a man and his son were camping on a shady spot overlooking Rock Springs Run. The sun was blazing, but it was cool under the sprawling oaks.

I lingered in camp, talking to the campers, and watched turtles play in the crystalline water. Canoes drifted by leisurely. I wondered how many people realized as they floated by that they were surrounded by the habitat of the Florida black bear.

I rested for an hour before starting the long hike back to my car. By the time I reached the car, twilight was approaching. The setting sun threw shafts of golden light through the trees, illuminating the branches of the oaks. The fragrance of pines drifted up from the floor of the forest.

I was exhausted from the hike, but I felt a sense of elation at having seen so many signs of bears. I thought back to the night the bear had crossed in front of our car. Cars are the leading killer of black bears in the Wekiva River Basin. Bears usually cross roads at night or early in the morning by blindly dashing across without regard to oncoming traffic. I wondered if the bear we had seen had made it safely to her home.

At the entrance to the reserve I read the words of Chief Seattle, written in 1884: "What happens to beasts will happen to man. All things are connected. If the great beasts are gone, men will surely die of a great loneliness of spirit."

Yes, I thought to myself, for the sake of all of us, I hope our bear did make it home.

A ROYAL
DILEMMA

*I*t seems that many people in America are experiencing a profound longing for the country. I see evidence of this in the proliferation of periodicals devoted to rural life. Magazines like *Countryside*, *Country Home*, and *Country Woman* appeal to a nostalgia for a simpler, more harmonious lifestyle. I suspect that many of the subscribers are urban folk, burned out on (but unable to escape) the rat race, who read the magazines as a kind of wish book—a way of vicariously going back to the land.

Although I already live in the country, this desire for the homely pleasures of the farm, and a longing for simplicity, made me want to do something that would bring me more in touch with the cycles of nature. So I decided to get a pig.

I'd been toying with the idea of raising livestock. I saw it as an opportunity to participate in the cycle of life in a more direct way. The economics of it seemed right. I was paying $2.50 a pound for pork chops. Why not get a small pig, I asked myself, raise it on feed and table scraps for a few months, have it butchered in the winter when it got to several hundred pounds, and put the meat in my freezer? Besides, commercially raised pork is force-fed, injected with steroids and other disagreeable substances. I could control the whole process and ensure that we were eating only the best pork.

So I got a baby Yorkshire pig, and as easy as that, I was in business. But in my quest to simplify my life, I found that it almost immmediately, and irrevocably, complicated it.

I put the little pig in a pen behind the house beneath a canopy of live oaks down by the lake. Having installed her in her new home, I looked into her dark, brown eyes and I noted her expression of bewilderment, then resignation. I must admit that she was a handsome pig, as pigs go. Her torso was firm and shapely, and she had a bright, pinkish complexion. She poked her little snout through the pen and nuzzled my hand with her wet nose. Her pink, floppy ears stood upright in anticipation as I brought her fresh water and a bowl of food.

My wife and I ransacked our minds for an appropriate name, although I sensed intuitively that it might be best not to name an animal that was destined for the dinner table. Wren noted her regal appearance, her bright, almost haughty look, and the way she stepped gingerly about the pen on her pointed hooves as if setting out for a grand ball in high heels.

"She's like a princess," I noted.

Our two cats, Sophocles (named for the Greek playwright) and Biscotti (Little Biscuits after the Tuscan cookie) came down to check out the intruder. As the four of us watched our new boarder gobble her food, I exclaimed, "I know what to name her."

"What?" Wren asked, as the cats looked away bored and petulant.

"Princess Diana."

"Perfect," Wren agreed. "We'll call her Princess Di."

So, with the snap of a finger, our humble lakeside home was transformed from the house of two struggling artists to the abode of royalty.

I took pleasure for the first two months in feeding and watering Princess Di, watching her grow with amazing rapidity from infant to teenager to young adult. I must admit that I did feel closer to the earth, to the cycles of nature. Waking in the early hours of the morning to bring feed to her brought me a certain inexpressible joy. The birds had begun their chatter and the sunrise over the lake turned the trees lining the shore a brilliant orange. Yes, the earth was a beautiful place, I philosophized.

I soon realized, however, that the Princess was not entirely happy with her castle, for she began to break out of the pen. One evening, as Wren and I sat in the living room listening to a recording of Leontyne Price sing arias from Puccini's *Madame Butterfly*, we heard an unexpected bass-baritone in the back yard. Startled, we turned to see our Princess Di staring into the window with a forlorn and lonely expression, as if she wished to join us. She bellowed in a tone that was heartbreaking.

After I put her back into her pen and returned to the living room, I could sense that the domestic atmosphere had changed. Wren had taken the record from the turntable and she glared at me with unmasked hostility.

"You're not going to, are you?" she asked.

I opened a book absently and pretended to read. "Going to what?" I said nonchalantly, not looking up.

The silence in the room hung heavy as wood smoke. Sophocles and Biscotti had come downstairs, and the three of them glared at me as if I were a criminal.

"You can't," Wren said emphatically.

I turned a page of my book and feigned disinterest. "I don't know what you're talking about."

Sophocles leaped up onto the arm of my chair and stared at me with a malicious, animal cruelty.

"I won't permit you to..." Wren began, then seemed to falter for a word, "...butcher that sweet little pig," and she began to weep.

So my dream of self-sufficiency was over. My desire to live closer to the land had cast me in the unlikely role of executioner. Still, I brought out all of the ammunition in my arsenal of logic.

"You never seem to object to buying meat in the grocery store," I argued lamely. "You eat hamburgers, don't you? And steak. You eat fish. They have feelings. What about plants? They're living creatures, too!"

But my arguments, as they say, fell on deaf ears.

It seems to me that a lot of people are perfectly willing to eat meat, as long as someone else pulls the trigger. Even vegetarians have staked out a high moral ground for themselves, despite forests being cleared for farmland, animals eradicated, and insects destroyed— all in the name of putting a lettuce-and-tomato salad on their tables.

Whereas I, in an attempt to live closer to the earth, had been indicted for intended butchery, tried by a jury of my peers (Wren, Sophocles, and Biscotti), and found guilty. And in that reversal of fortune that often attends life, the condemned had been suddenly set free, and the previously free had been just as suddenly condemned.

So Princess Di has been granted a stay. I even let her out of her cell to root around in the yard to her heart's content, destroying my flower beds if she so pleases. Such are the extremes that the guilty will go to in order to relieve their sense of guilt.

What had seemed two months ago to be a financially

sound investment, has become a financial liability. But there is still that joy when the sun is rising over the lake and the mourning doves are cooing. I go down to give the Princess fresh water and feed. She looks up to me with the innocence of true fraternity and nuzzles my hand with her wet nose.

Though I am on better terms with the felines in my house, there is still an awkwardness, and I am met with stares of contempt if I even so much as suggest that some night we might have pork chops for dinner.

A CRUISE THROUGH THE LAKES

Our guide cuts the engine as we drift silently toward two cypress trees. The air is still and the water of the lake shimmers beneath the afternoon sun. I lift my binoculars to my eyes and focus on the enormous nest of branches and twigs at the top of one of the trees. Two ospreys lift their heads above the rim of the nest.

I began this outdoor adventure just three blocks from Winter Park's chic Park Avenue at the foot of Morse Boulevard on Lake Osceola. Under the spreading canopy of live oaks, I leave the city behind and step into an older, gentler world. I'm on the famous "Scenic Boat Tour" of Winter Park's chain of lakes.

Stan Smith greets me under the covered dock where the tour boats are moored. Originally from North Carolina, Stan has worked for the Scenic Boat Tour for twenty years. He gives me some background information on the operation.

The Scenic Boat Tour was established in Winter Park in 1938. Now in its fifty-third year, the tour takes visitors on a one-hour excursion through Lake Osceola, Lake Virginia, and Lake Maitland, offering a behind-the-scenes look at Winter Park, where graceful mansions overlook tropical shorelines.

Mr. Smith telephones the current owners of the tour, Wanda and Frank Salerno. Wanda agrees to come down and give me some more information on the tour.

In the meantime, our tour boat has arrived. I climb aboard the sixteen-seat pontoon boat and embark on an expedition on Winter Park's lovely waterways. The passengers are a mix of young and old, tourists and long-time residents.

Our skipper, Dick Black, expertly guides the craft through Lake Osceola, pointing to the right at an expansive lawn with statues among the palm trees and shrubbery. "This is the Polasek Galleries," he tells us. "Albin Polasek was a twenty-one year old Czechoslovakian woodcarver when he came to this country in 1904 to study art. He retired at the pinnacle of his career as the curator of sculpture at the Chicago Institute of Art, and built his retirement studio at 633 Osceola Avenue. The gallery is open to the public."

The sky is clear as we follow the shoreline. One beautiful home after another sits placidly beneath moss-drenched live oaks. Our skipper points out the white snail eggs on the stems of water lilies and hyacinths growing along the lush shore. We pass the winter home of Harry Sinclair, the founder of Sinclair Oil, and take note of the two-hundred-year-old cypress tree on the property.

"The tree to our left," our skipper continues, "is an example of a Southern longleaf yellow pine. This was the mainstay of the economy from 1880 when a sawmill was built on Lake Virginia. The canals were opened up to tow the logs from the lakes to the sawmill."

We pass under the Osceola Bridge by way of a narrow canal choked with banana trees and an overhanging camphor tree. A stand of Calcutta bamboo leaning over the canal adds to the exotic flavor of the adventure. On the banks grow red Turk's cap, blue morning glories, white Queen Anne's lace, and a wild asparagus plant.

We emerge on Lake Virginia.

"A lot of bass fisherman enjoy fishing for big bass on this lake," the skipper tells us. "There are also gar, eel, catfish, and crappie."

Off to the left is Lake Mizell. At sixty acres, it's the smallest lake of the Winter Park chain. The channel that leads to this lake is too small for our boat. Across the lake we see Rollins College, with the Moroccan-style steeple of Knowles Chapel soaring above the tree line.

"The Genius Estate is off to our left," says the skipper. "About 250 acres were purchased in 1904 for about $1.25 an acre."

"Wow," I say to the person next to me. "I'd like to have gotten in on that deal."

"On the property," he continues, "there are over one hundred pairs of peacocks roaming freely."

We can hear the loud screams of the birds. On the lawn of the residence, pairs of peacocks strut about, trailing their rainbow of tail feathers behind.

A pair of wood ducks flies overhead and a blue heron takes off out of the reeds. Wood duck nests are placed on poles and in the trees around the estate.

Our skipper starts the engine and we motor across the slalom course of the Rollins College skiing team to the southern shore of the lake.

Cutting the engine and drifting, Dick Black tells us: "The timber industry was the mainstay of the economy from 1880 to about World War I. Then two things happened. The railroads had come into the center part of the state, and the demand for citrus grew tremendously. Subsequently, the landowners converted their land from timber to citrus, so that they could have a cash crop every year rather than having to wait thirty or forty years to cut the timber. Eventually, the grove owners sold their land for development and bought more land in other parts of the state."

The skipper eases the boat along the shoreline and

points to the land. "The ridge off to our left is interesting topographically, because it forms a watershed divide between north and south Florida at this part of the state. All the rainfall that falls to the south of that ridge flows into the city of Orlando's lakes and then into the Kissimmee River Basin south to Lake Okeechobee. But all the rainfall that occurs on this side flows northward into this chain of lakes and eventually into the St. Johns River Basin and then to the Atlantic Ocean."

He noses the boat along the shoreline. We admire the many magnificent homes as we drift past Rollins College. An anhinga stands on a dock, drying its feathers. Dick explains that the anhinga, or snake bird, does not have natural oils on its feathers as do most water birds. Their feathers become saturated with water and the bird must sit in the sun and extend its wings to dry them.

We skim across the lake and back through the channel connecting Lake Virginia and Lake Osceola. At the dock, we pick up Wanda Salerno, owner of the Scenic Boat Tour, before continuing our journey into Lake Maitland.

As we speed across the water toward Lake Maitland, a flock of mallard ducks flies overhead. Wanda Salerno tells me that the Melloon family began the first Scenic Boat Tour on January 1, 1938. They ran the tour for nineteen years.

A Bermuda-style house sits on a point of land extending into the lake. We wind our way through the bends and turns of the Venetian Canal. A palm tree extends over the canal on our right as the boat knocks and scrapes against the narrow sides of the canal and under the Palmer Avenue bridge. We emerge from the canopy of growth shading the canal into the bright sunshine over Lake Maitland.

Kraft Azalea Park, on our right, is one of the city parks of Winter Park. In the distance, I can make out the red roof line of the old Alabama Hotel.

"It played host in the 1930's and '40's to many famous personalities," the skipper tells us, pointing to the old hotel that is now a condominium. "Margaret Mitchell, author of *Gone With The Wind*, stayed there just thirty days before her tragic auto accident."

We pass the Isle of Sicily, an area of beautiful homes on a piece of land shaped roughly like the Island of Sicily off the Italian peninsula.

"How long have you and your husband been running the Scenic Boat Tour?" I ask Wanda Salerno.

"Ten years in February," she says. "We thoroughly enjoy it. We've had our share of ups and downs. In 1981, we had a drought and we were on this one lake for five months. And this year we were on this one lake for two months. The drought had lowered the water level in the canals so that the boats could not go through."

The skipper cuts the engine as we drift toward two cypress trees. "Osprey are a large member of the fishhawk family, and an endangered species," says Dick Black. He points to the nest. "You can see one of this year's young up on the nest."

Looking at the bird poking its head out of the huge nest, I find it hard to believe that we are in the heart of Winter Park.

"We have six boats," Wanda continues. "We can handle up to one hundred people at a time. We do private cruises by appointment. We've had weddings, rehearsal dinners." She looks at me slyly. "We've done just about everything there is to do on these boats."

"Who takes the Scenic Boat Tour?"

"We have a lot of business from the United Kingdom. But people from Winter Park take the tour, too. We sometimes see the same people every month. Some people have a lot of company or just know many people and they want them to see the tour. I had a German couple and an English couple tell me that the reason they came was that their friends told them if they were ever in the Orlando area, they should go on the Scenic Boat Tour."

A fury of dark clouds has gathered to the north as we motor back across Lake Maitland. The trip has been relaxing and enlightening—and for just five dollars for adults and two-fifty for children, it's a real bargain if you're looking for outdoor activity within the Orlando metropolitan area.

I agree with the folks from England and Germany. If you are ever in the Orlando area, take the Scenic Boat Tour.

SUMMER OF THE
MOON LAUNCH

One warm summer morning, my brother Tom and I stood at the end of a wooden pier that reaches into the lake in front of our home in Lake County and waited with anticipation for an event which we hardly believed was possible. At 9:32 a.m., on July 16, 1969, we watched the contrail of Apollo 11 pierce the cloudless blue sky of Florida.

This was in the days before Disney World had remade Central Florida. The only world we knew was rural Florida—an area of citrus groves, pickup trucks, crystalline lakes, and warm, quiet evenings. Yes, times were simpler then.

In retrospect, it strikes me as particularly ironic that two country boys like Tom and me, who rarely strayed farther than the woods that surrounded our parents' orange grove, watched as the first men to walk on the surface of the moon were shot skyward from Launch Complex 39, less than eighty miles from where we stood, to the moon, nearly a quarter of a million miles away. What we witnessed that morning in 1969 was the beginning of a new era. Standing on the end of the dock, our faces turned upward in wonder, it was almost impossible to believe that we were watching from our back yard the first men who were to walk on the face of the moon being blasted into space. Historic moments always occurred elsewhere. But this was one of the greatest achievements in the history of mankind. And it started in Central Florida. We were proud.

Still, we were told by a group of tobacco-chewing grove workers that the moon walk which we watched on TV three days later was a hoax dreamed up by the federal government for dubious reasons and staged in a sandpit somewhere outside of Zellwood.

Even we could never have imagined back then that a hometown boy would play a part in the unfolding drama of man's exploration of space. David Walker, who had graduated from Eustis High School in 1962, would pilot the orbiter Discovery in November 1984 on its mission to deploy two communications satellites and retrieve two other disabled ones.

At the time, Tom and I were both aspiring scientists. I was thirteen and he was fifteen. I had acquired a chemistry set for Christmas, and we had been running a series of experiments on the local fauna.

We were also devotees of the model-rocket craze. The week before, we had successfully launched a palmetto bug 2,000 feet into the air, and as the little parachute opened, we watched sadly as our rocket drifted out of sight to land eventually in some distant lake or orange grove on the other side of the county.

Tonight, I sit out on the same dock thinking about the events of twenty-three years ago. I've watched many launchings from this dock, now rickety with age. A full moon rises above the horizon and casts an amber river of light across the quiet lake. I'm twenty-three years older now. Many things have changed.

Three days after the launch of Apollo 11, I watched with my family as Neil Armstrong pointed out to more than 500 million TV viewers the plaque that the crew had placed at the landing spot on the moon. "Here men from the planet Earth first set foot upon the moon July 1969 A.D. We came in peace for all mankind."

I find myself musing on the events of that summer of the moon launch, for they seem to constitute a particularly apt metaphor for all that Florida is becoming. Like a couple of country kids witnessing the dawn of the space age in their own back yard, an unprepared Florida is witnessing a dramatic explosion of population, and its subsequent problems, as it hurtles recklessly toward the 21st century. Not the least of those problems is the destruction of Florida's precious environment.

I was born in Florida in 1956. There were less than four million people in the state. Today, the figure approaches thirteen million. It is now the fourth most populous state in the union and, according to projections made by the University of Florida, the population by the year 2000 could exceed sixteen million.

The tremendous demand that this places upon the resources of the state cannot be overestimated. In addition to a critical need for improved roads, schools, and an adequate tax base, it is equally important that we protect Florida's unique and fragile natural environment. On the same lake where Tom and I watched in awe as Apollo 11 was blasted to the moon, we have watched with dismay the water level drop as much as twenty feet.

Tom, now a doctoral candidate at Florida State, and I have adjusted to the demands of a society far from our world of slow, hot days by the lake watching alligators slither through the tea-colored water. We will never forget those languid, subtropical nights of childhood, alive with the voices of frogs and cicadas singing from moss-draped oaks. But we have experienced pain in our adjustment.

Sitting out here tonight listening to the whippoor-wills call to each other across the lake and looking up at the pockmarked lunar surface, I worry about our Florida.

Like its sons and daughters, Florida will also adjust,

but not without the pain of crowded highways, pollution, increasing demands on the environment, and a last farewell to a way of life that is gone forever.

"The roots of all living things are tied together," say the Lacandon Maya of the Mexican rain forest. It's true. I know that if we destroy Florida's environment, we will eventually destroy our globe. I hate to think so, but maybe someday the only evidence left of the human race will be a plaque up there on the eerie, windless surface of the moon that reads ironically: "We came in peace for all mankind."

NATIVE'S
EUPHORIA

I sit on the porch swing sipping sweet iced tea from a tall glass. The aroma of orange blossoms lingers in the breeze that rattles the palm fronds in the trees behind my house. I watch a kingfisher diving for fish in the placid lake, and remember my years of exile.

It took five years of living in the cold cities of the North to realize that the Florida I call home and the images of Florida conjured by most snow-bound residents of the northern latitudes are two very different places. When I would describe my home in Central Florida—ten acres on a lake near the edge of the Ocala National Forest—to Northern friends, they were incredulous. Most of them had been to Florida. But what they had seen—suburban sprawl, gaudy tourist attractions, plastic, neon and asphalt—was nothing like the Florida that I described.

Florida, where I was born and raised, the home I fled from and returned to, is an area of lakes, rivers, springs, creeks, orange groves, and jungle. The Ocala National Forest, the only subtropical forest in America, is alive with wildlife: deer, turkeys, black bears, alligators, wild hogs, bobcats. It is a land of slow, hot evenings when frogs, crickets, and other creatures create a tremendous racket. A rural area in a mostly urban state, it is a land of pickup trucks, Bar-B-Q stands, crackers, blacks, retirees, and the remains of a crippled citrus industry.

While many people in Florida are relatively recent arrivals to the state, I grew up with people who have lived in Florida for generations. Their grandparents homesteaded vast tracts of land from which they hacked out citrus groves. Here the Old South meets the tropics and the values of the South still linger. Yet it is not the South. It is Florida. And Florida has always been and always will be, I hope, a different kind of place.

There is one special place near my home that is among the most beautiful spots in our state. Located approximately an hour and a half north of Orlando off State Road 19, Alexander Springs is one of numerous springs in the Ocala National Forest. Adjacent to the spring are facilities for camping, picnicking, swimming, and hiking.

Although most visitors come by car and park at the national park entrance, I like to put my canoe in at the bridge on County Road 445 near Astor and paddle upriver to the spring. There is nothing so peaceful as this quiet creek just before dawn. A mist hangs over the water as the sun peeks through the lush shoreline of pine trees and sabal palms. The aroma of pine needles wafts across the stream, and the splash of an alligator slipping off the bank into the water scares up a blue heron that wings its way into the rising sun. This is a scene I have witnessed hundreds of times and of which I never tire.

The creek originates in the "boil" of Alexander Springs, a thirty-foot-deep cavity from which the water bubbles. Alexander is classified as a "first magnitude" spring which pumps over 80 million gallons of water a day from the underground aquifer. This water remains a constant 72 degrees throughout the year.

In the area around the spring the Timucuan Indians followed a traditional way of life, gathering shells, hunting, and fishing. Remnants of their culture in the form of arrowheads and shell mounds can still be found along the Timucuan Indian Trail that leads off into the dense forest. The trail is posted with interpretive markers that give the names of various plants and explain their significance in the lives of the Timucuan people.

I land my canoe near the spring and swim over the boil with a mask and snorkel. Through the incredibly clear water, I see schools of mullet (which come upstream from the ocean), bass, bream, and many other fish. The boil is aquamarine, and the white, sandy bottom of the spring glows as if it were phosphorescent.

The boil is popular among scuba divers. On the bottom of the boil are limestone caverns that lure curious divers into their recesses. Some of these divers have never returned to the surface. I am told that they develop a condition known as nitrogen narcosis, in which the diver becomes disoriented and loses consciousness. But other people say that the divers experience a euphoria down that deep. Awed by the beauty that surrounds them, they find themselves unable, or unwilling, to return to the surface.

Such has been my love affair with the subtropical latitudes of Florida.

As a child, I daydreamed of the world outside the confines of these lakes and hammocks, sand hills, and forests. At the first opportunity, I left to find that world. But I carried the images of my home with me, through the frozen reaches of the Midwest, and the industrial sprawl of the Northeast, and I knew that one day I would come home. Now I am back, living on the same ten acres where my father planted his roots half a century ago. Now that I am here again, I find myself struck with the diver's euphoria.

I do not know if I will ever surface.

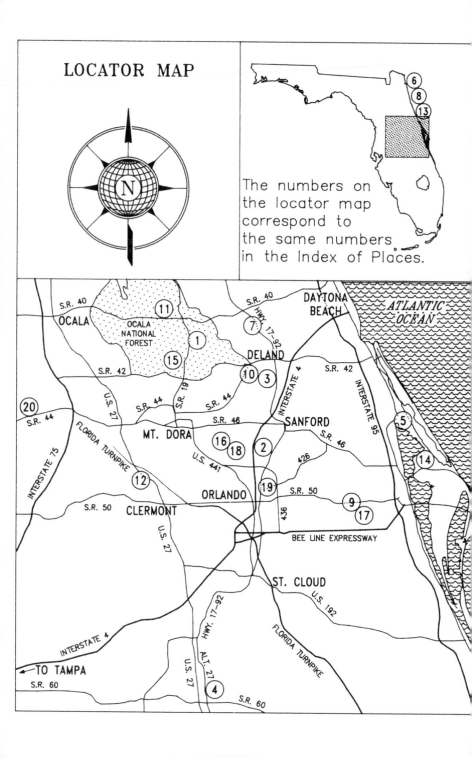

LOCATOR MAP

The numbers on the locator map correspond to the same numbers in the Index of Places.

INDEX
OF PLACES

Below is an alphabetized list of places mentioned in the book, as well as directions and telephone numbers, so that you too can explore the natural beauty of Florida. The number heading each place corresponds to the same number on the accompanying locator map. To read more about each place, please turn to the page number accompanying the title of each chapter.

1. ALEXANDER SPRINGS RECREATION AREA
Near Altoona
Located approximately 1 1/2 hours
north of Orlando on County Road 445,
off of State Roads 19 and 40.
(904) 669-3522
Page 124: Native's Euphoria

2. BIG TREE PARK
General Hutchinson Parkway
Longwood, FL
Located 1 mile west of U.S. Highway 17-92 in Longwood.
(407) 323-9615
Page 94: An Afternoon With the Senator

3. BLUE SPRING STATE PARK
2100 West French Ave.
Orange City, FL 32763
Located about 25 miles north of Orlando
and 2 miles west of Orange City
off of I-4 and U.S. Highway 17-92.
(904) 775-3663
Page 44: Blue Spring

4. BOK TOWER GARDENS
Lake Wales, FL   33859-3810
Located about 3 miles north of
Lake Wales off of U.S. Highway 27.
(813) 676-1408
Page 54: A Little Bit of Heaven

5. CANAVERAL NATIONAL SEASHORE
2532 Garden St.
Titusville, FL 32796
Northern access point located
at New Smyrna Beach on State Road A1A.
Southern access point located on
State Road 402 in Titusville.
Visitor Center: (904) 428-3384
Headquarters: (407) 267-1110
Page 10: Turtle Watch

6. CASTILLO DE SAN MARCOS
NATIONAL MONUMENT
1 Castillo Drive
St. Augustine, FL
(904) 829-6506
Page 65: Florida History

7. DeLEON SPRINGS STATE RECREATION AREA
P.O. Box 1338
DeLeon Springs, FL 32030
Located north of DeLand off
of U.S. Highway 17 (Ponce DeLeon Blvd.).
(904) 985-4212
Page 79: Fountain of Youth

8. FORT MATANZAS NATIONAL MONUMENT
Near Summer Haven
Located 14 miles south of St. Augustine
on State Road A1A. Ferry boat runs
9 a.m.-4:30 p.m., weather permitting.
(904)-471-0116
Page 65: Florida History

9. GATOR JUNGLE
Clabrook Farm, Inc.
26205 East Highway 50
Christmas, FL 32709
Located 6 miles west of Titusville and
17 miles east of Orlando on State Road 50.
(407) 568-2885
Page 19: Gator Jungle

10. HONTOON ISLAND STATE PARK
c/o Blue Spring State Park
2100 West French Ave.
Orange City, FL 32763
Island is located 6 miles west of
DeLand, off State Road 44
(904) 775-3663
Hontoon Island State Park: (904) 736-5309
Page 34: Island of the Owl Clan

11. JUNIPER SPRINGS RECREATION AREA
17147 East Highway 40
Silver Springs, FL   32688
Located 22 miles east of
Silver Springs on State Road 40
in the Ocala National Forest.
District Ranger: (904) 625-2520
Canoe Rental: (904) 625-2808
Page 25: Juniper Springs Run

12. LAKERIDGE WINERY & VINEYARDS
19239 U.S. Highway 27 North
Clermont, FL   34711-9025
Located on U.S. Highway 27, 2 miles south of
Florida's Turnpike, 6 miles north of
State Road 50, near Clermont.
(904) 394-8627
1-800-476-VINE (Toll-free)
Page 88: Like Good Wine

13. MARINELAND
State Road A1A
Marineland, FL
Located 18 miles south of St. Augustine
on State Road A1A.
(904) 471-1111
Page 65: Florida History

14. MERRITT ISLAND NATIONAL WILDLIFE REFUGE
P.O. Box 6504
Titusville, FL 32782
Information Center located on State Road 402,
4 miles east of Titusvile.
(407) 867-0667
Page 70: Mad Dogs and Englishmen

15. OCALA NATIONAL FOREST
Pittman Visitor Center
45621 State Road 19
Altoona, FL 32702
Visitor Center located 3 miles north of State Road 42.
Nearly 430,000 acres located
east of Ocala between the
Oklawaha and St. Johns rivers.
(904) 669-3153 (Seminole district ranger)
(904) 625-2520 (Lake George district ranger)
(904) 681-7265 (USDA-Forest Service supervisor)
Page 39: The Disappearing Woodpecker

16. ROCK SPRINGS RUN STATE RESERVE
Route 1 Box 365D
Sorrento, FL 32776
Located off of County Road 433. I-4 to Exit 51,
west for 7 miles on State Road 46, then left on County Road 433,
which dead-ends at entrance to reserve.
(904) 383-3311
Page 103: Bear Crossing

17. TOSOHATCHEE STATE RESERVE
3365 Taylor Creek Road
Christmas, FL 32709
Located 20 miles east of Orlando off of State Road 50.
(407) 568-5893
Page 59: A Bird in the Bush

18. WEKIWA SPRINGS STATE PARK
1800 Wekiwa Circle
Apopka, FL 32712
Located on Wekiva Springs Road
off State Roads 434 or 436.
(407) 884-2009
Page 5: Wekiwa Trail

19. WINTER PARK CHAIN OF LAKES
Morse Boulevard
Winter Park, FL
Scenic Boat Tour leaves on the hour from 10 a.m. to 4 p.m.
from the east end of Morse Boulevard on Lake Osceola.
(407) 644-4056
Page 114: A Cruise Through the Lakes

20. WITHLACOOCHEE RIVER
Airboat Tours
Located on State Road 44, 8 miles
west of I-75, Exit 66, 6 miles east of Inverness.
(904) 726-6060 (Airboat Tours)
Page 74: *The Withlacoochee With Wild Bill*

ABOUT THE AUTHOR

Jonathan Harrington was born in Florida in 1956. He received a Master of Fine Arts degree from the University of Iowa Writers' Workshop in 1983. In 1989, he co-edited *New Visions: Fiction by Florida Writers*, published by Arbiter Press. "Tropical Son," which appears monthly in *METRO* Magazine, won the coveted Gold "Charlie" Award from the Florida Magazine Association for best column of the year in 1990. Currently, Mr. Harrington teaches writing at the University of Central Florida, in Orlando.

His poetry and fiction have appeared in numerous magazines in the U.S. and abroad, including *Green River Review*, *Poetry Ireland Review*, *Kentucky Poetry Review*, *South Florida Poetry Review*, *The Spectator*, *Black Bear Review*, *English Journal*, *Skylight*, and *Fiction Quarterly*. His poetry has been awarded an Iowa Arts Grant Award and has been featured on public radio. His nonfiction has appeared in *Southern Exposure*, *The Daily Iowan*, *The Orlando Sentinel*, *Florida Review*, *Pencil Press Quarterly*, *Rollins Alumni Record*, and *Facing South*, a syndicated column published in more than 100 newspapers.

ORDER FORM

I would like to have additional copies of this book,

TROPICAL SON

BY JONATHAN HARRINGTON

Please send _____ copies to the address below:

Name_____

Address_____

City_____ State____ Zip_____

Enclosed please find check or money order in the amount of _____ that includes $9.95 for each book plus $2.60 for postage, tax, and mailing for each book.

Please mail to:
NewTech Publications
1330 Palmetto Ave.
Winter Park, FL 32789

To order by phone using Visa or MasterCard, please call (407) 629-2393.